Brandon Sch...

111 Places
in Philadelphia
That You Must
Not Miss

Photographs by Lucy Baber

emons:

To Jeffrey, whose ears have spent the last two years enduring more "interesting" Philly trivia than he cared for, surely, but who never stopped smiling and nodding.

MIX
Paper from
responsible sources
FSC® C043106
FSC
www.fsc.org

© Emons Verlag GmbH
All rights reserved
© Photographs by Lucy Baber, except see p. 238
© Cover Icon: private
Layout: Eva Kraskes, based on a design
by Lübbeke | Naumann | Thoben
Maps: altancicek.design, www.altancicek.de
Basic cartographical information from Openstreetmap,
© OpenStreetMap-Mitwirkende, OdbL
Editing: Karen E. Seiger
Printing and binding: Grafisches Centrum Cuno, Calbe
Printed in Germany 2022
ISBN 978-3-7408-1376-5
First edition

Guidebooks for Locals & Experienced Travelers
Join us in uncovering new places around the world at
www.111places.com

Foreword

Philadelphia's story begins long before the American Revolution, with a wealth of European and Native American histories predating both 1776 and the city's official founding in 1682. Philly's Colonial remnants are extensively documented in countless travel guides. They are well worth exploring, but it's time to pay more attention to the lesser-told tales of those who came both before and after, leaving behind remnants of dazzling contributions to fields stretching from arts and sciences to murder and mayhem, most of which are still scattered around the city today, hiding in plain sight.

America's first cult leader lived in a cave here, and the country's first famous serial killer was hanged here. William and Letitia Still sheltered Harriet Tubman in a house that still stands on Delhi Street. An empress is buried in a barely marked grave next to a sidewalk on 13th Street. The list of impressive individuals who have passed through Philadelphia is long.

Philly's more ordinary residents are what make it extraordinary today. From swing dance and burlesque groups to cutting-edge play-spaces for children and an inexplicable box full of free Shrek merch for anyone, Philadelphians have a penchant for the unique and a knack for sharing their gifts with their neighbors.

Even the museums here are different. Yes, there are world-class collections like those at the Philadelphia Museum of Art and the Barnes Foundation (though even these are home to often-untold stories worthy of a spotlight), but Philly also boasts a Neon Museum, an Insectarium, and, of course, a Mummers Museum.

Within these pages, you'll uncover the fascinating details of everything mentioned here and so much more, along with tips on where to find them and the best ways to experience each, discovering exactly why there's no other city in America that's home to residents more fiercely proud of their hometown.

111 Places

1 Adrian Balboa's Grave

A real grave for a fictional character

Few characters are as firmly entrenched in the Philadelphia psyche as Rocky Balboa, so it's understandable that some may wonder whether he was a real person. He was not (though his story was based on the career of the very real heavyweight Chuck Wepner). Though a bronze statue cast for a scene in *Rocky III* now stands permanently at the base of the Philadelphia Museum of Art staircase, better known as the "Rocky Steps" and ranked by *Screen Junkies* as the second most famous filming location in the world, there's a more confounding remnant of the Rocky legacy lurking elsewhere in the city that loves him so.

From the main gate on Ridge Avenue, turn left immediately after entering Laurel Hill Cemetery and follow the fence until you encounter the gravestone of Adrian Balboa nestled neatly between two shrubs. Set just enough apart to visibly stand out from other markers, it's easy to spot and even bears engraved birth and death dates, like just almost any other stone in the cemetery.

Adrian's story (ahem, life) ends after the events of *Rocky V*, and her death is made apparent through the appearance of this gravestone in *Rocky Balboa*, but this isn't quite her first marker. The original prop was constructed of Styrofoam, but Sylvester Stallone apparently found it too tacky for use and ordered this proper memorial carved for his fictional character's beloved wife.

Though the setting looks nothing like the hilltop you saw in the opening minutes and final, tear-jerking scene of *Rocky Balboa*, this is still the authentic prop stone used in the film and left behind at Laurel Hill Cemetery, where it has presumably found its own final resting place. Far from the never-ending tourist lines crowding the Rocky statue and summiting the 72 steps of the art museum from dawn till beyond dusk daily, you'll find Adrian's grave to be, bizarrely, a more authentic Rocky experience.

ADRIAN
BALBOA

MARCH 10 1950
JANUARY 11 2002

Address 3822 Ridge Avenue, Philadelphia, PA 19132, +1 (215) 228-8200,
www.laurelhillphl.com, info@laurelhillphl.com | Getting there Bus 61 to Ridge Avenue &
W Clearfield Street | Hours See website for seasonal hours | Tip Just one "plot" to the left
of Adrian's grave, you'll find the grave of another, lesser-known Rocky character, Adrian's
brother Paul "Paulie" Pennino (3822 Ridge Avenue, www.laurelhillphl.com).

2 __ Albert Einstein's Pipe
You've seen it in photos, now see it in person

While the largest populations of Jewish Americans are found in New York and New Jersey, Philadelphia is home to the Weitzman National Museum of American Jewish History. The only museum of its focus in the world started as a modest collection of 40 items gathered during the United States Bicentennial to represent the Jewish American immigrant experience. It is now a collection of more than 30,000 objects sharing space in an eye-popping, five-story, glass structure on Independence Mall.

Supporting its mission to share the story of American Jews with everyone, the museum's "Only in America" Gallery is admission free, so pop in any time you're passing by, even if you don't have time to explore the rest of the museum at the moment. Among this easily-accessed collection is Albert Einstein's iconic smoking pipe. Though Einstein stopped smoking as he got older, he kept his signature pipe for the familiar sensation.

Upstairs you'll find more than 1,000 artifacts in permanent and temporary exhibitions, helping to illuminate the diversity of the American Jewish experience over more than 300 years. Each new exhibition also brings a series of programs for more intimate interactions with its themes, including concerts, lectures, storytelling, and films, bolstering the museum's mission to both educate and celebrate Jewish American history with both Jews and non-Jews alike.

Part of the museum's permanent education efforts, more than a dozen high-tech, interactive installations offer hands-on engagement with the stories of Jewish American immigrants ranging from the earliest to the most prominent, and the Weitzman's affiliation with the Smithsonian Institution brings regular loans from the group's collection of more than 140 million additional pieces. Saturday tickets can't be purchased at the door due to Shabbat, so purchase in advance if this is your target day.

Address 101 S Independence Mall East, Philadelphia, PA 19106, +1 (215) 923-3811, www.theweitzman.org, enews@nmajhg.org | Getting there Subway to 5th Street Independence Hall (Market–Frankford Line); Bus 17, 33, 38 to 5th & Market Streets | Hours Fri–Sun 10am–5pm | Tip The Mikveh Israel Cemetery has been the permanent resting place of many prominent Jewish Philadelphians since 1740 (831 Spruce Street, www.mikvehisrael.org).

3 America's Best Bathroom

It's just outside Philadelphia, and it's alive

Just as there's a national day for everything, it seems there's also an award for almost anything, and that includes public restrooms. In 2014, Longwood Gardens was voted home of America's Best Restroom in an annual public contest hosted by Cintas (who awarded a complimentary deep cleaning as part of the grand prize). You're most likely aware of Longwood, and you've probably visited – it is the most visited public garden in America, after all. But if you haven't sought out its number one bathroom, you've been missing out.

So, what could make a public restroom so special you'd want to spend *more* time there? Like just about every attraction at Longwood Gardens, other than the famous fountains and 10,010-pipe organ, it's alive. Well, part of it is. Flanking the curved hall that hosts Longwood's restrooms is a wraparound living wall of woodland plants that covers the space, ceiling to floor, in living greenery that may give you the sense you've headed off to the woods for nature's call. The 4,200 square feet of continuous, 12-foot-tall vertical gardens are rife with ferns (at least five varieties, all named for animals from kangaroo to squirrel) and punctuated by philodendron, spider plants, and more.

A glass ceiling provides ample sunlight for the visually stunning space, and pests are managed by a fascinating team of thousands – they're other insects and mites released by Longwood throughout the year to prey on pests, and pose no threat to the plants or humans. Some of them even help pollinate, keeping the walls all the greener. And don't worry: you're unlikely to see this special force of friendly critters.

Nearly 50,000 plants are maintained on this largest living wall in North America, but the bathrooms behind are "green," too. They have heated floors, vented dome ceilings, and use 63% less water per flush than standard toilets.

Address 1001 Longwood Road, Kennett Square, PA 19348, +1 (610) 388-1000, www.longwoodgardens.org, questions@longwoodgardens.org | Getting there By car, take I-95 S to Exit 3A to US-322W | Hours See website for seasonal hours | Tip Practically bordering Longwood Gardens, Galer Estate Vineyard and Winery offers tastings on Friday and Saturday. Feel free to bring a picnic lunch (700 Folly Hill Road, Kennett Square, www.galerestate.com).

4 Assembly

The swankiest rooftop in town

Hotels are not just for out-of-towners, and the savviest city residents know exactly which ones boast the best restaurants and rooftops for an elevated (literally) removal from a stressful workday or dull routine. Quiet corners and secret enclaves can be welcome relief for these brief moments of staycation escapism, but it can be equally refreshing to recharge your romance with your hometown by hitting the heart of what makes it most famous. In Philly, this is best accomplished at Assembly, the rooftop bar of The Logan Hotel.

Sure, Philadelphia has plenty of famous streets and enough historical monuments to fill another book entirely, but the Philly view known 'round the world, from local news to internationally broadcast parades, is that of the Philadelphia Museum of Art at the end of the Benjamin Franklin Parkway. From atop The Logan, you'll not only catch a sweeping view of this stunner in the distance, but you'll also be surrounded by the icons of Logan Circle, including The Franklin Institute, The Free Library (see ch. 16), The Academy of Natural Sciences, and the Swann Memorial Fountain in the center of the circle itself.

In summer, the cozy couches surrounding fire pits on the outdoor deck are *the* spot for frozen cocktails and sunset views, but the ceiling-to-floor glass walls of Assembly make it a year-round hotspot regardless of weather. Reconnect with your roots through locally-inspired cocktails with names like "Down the Shore" and "It's Always Sunny," or dive directly into the rooftop bar's signature sip, champagne, perfect for celebrating anything from a promotion to a well-deserved moment of self-care. There aren't a lot of gimmicks, OMG-moments, or fly-by-night trends here (though take advantage of pop-up collabs if you catch one). It's simple Philadelphia sophistication with constant reminders of why you love Philly in the first place.

Address 1840 Benjamin Franklin Parkway, Philadelphia, PA 19103, +1 (215) 783-4171, www.assemblyrooftop.com | Getting there Bus 32, 33 to 19th & Cherry Streets | Hours Daily 4pm–midnight | Tip Both the hotel and circle are named for Philadelphia statesman James Logan, whose 3,000-volume library has been acquired by The Library Company of Philadelphia, which you can explore (1314 Locust Street, www.librarycompany.org).

5 __ Baleroy Mansion

Maybe a little too haunted

If you're someone who prefers a tidy ending to every story, you might want to skip this one. Beyond a mere haunted house from which you can simply walk away, Baleroy Mansion was once home to a piece of furniture with the alleged power to kill – and you may be sitting on it now. But let's not get ahead of ourselves.

This is a private home, and you can't go in it. But you can certainly take a short trip to Chestnut Hill to marvel at its exterior from the street. Its mature landscaping and long, stone-walled driveway ooze a cemeterial vibe that may just give you the creeps as you ponder the events that have unfolded within. Start by understanding that this 32-room mansion wasn't constructed until the early 20th-century. But note that it was soon purchased by the Easby family, who sailed with William Penn aboard the *Welcome* and count among their ancestors seven signers of the Declaration of Independence, as well as General George Meade, hero of the Battle of Gettysburg.

Legend holds that the first owner murdered his wife here, kicking off a cascade of mysterious illnesses and deaths that have never been explained. The youngest Easby son died of an unknown illness a few years after moving in, and his ghost is among the specters reported to inhabit the home still. Staff have been spooked, a minister was hit with a flying pot, and Easby family members claimed to have been pranked regularly by spirits through the generations. Even Thomas Jefferson is said to haunt the dining room occasionally.

Still, the most fascinating element of Baleroy is the 200-year-old "chair of death" that has claimed the lives of at least four unsuspecting sitters before the last Easby to live here banned anyone from using it. After his death in 2005, the antique contents of Baleroy were auctioned off, and the current location of this chair remains a potentially fatal mystery today.

Address 111 W Mermaid Lane, Philadelphia, PA 19118 | Getting there Bus 23 to Germantown Avenue & W Mermaid Lane | Hours Unrestricted from the outside only | Tip General Meade also died in Philadelphia, though without mystery and intrigue. A historical marker notes his 1872 death near Rittenhouse Square (1836 Delancey Place, www.hmdb.org).

6 Barnes Foundation

Black culture among the impressionists

The Barnes Foundation is world renowned for its staggering collection of impressionist, post-impressionist, and modern art, but the under-sung African art collection that enchanted Albert Barnes is worth a visit entirely on its own.

To begin, accept that a visit to this museum will be unlike most. Paintings are not starkly isolated upon white walls, but woven together in vignettes of artistic dialog highlighting theme, form, and the conversations that seem to leap from their chance meeting. Barnes never intended his collection as a museum, but rather a school for invited art students. Though the collection was contentiously relocated from Lower Merion (check out the documentary *The Art of the Steal* for plenty of insight here), each room and vignette has been replicated exactly as Barnes originally arranged. It continues to serve an education mission while also opening the collection to the public.

Do check out as much of this $25-billion collection as you can, but pay special attention to two rooms on the second floor: Room 20 and Room 22. While amassing his astonishing collection, Barnes was among the first to recognize African art as advanced, not "primitive" as his contemporaries deemed. He was determined to have the world's best collection of African sculpture, which he believed to be the "purest expression of three-dimensional form." The 123 pieces he collected are today arranged primarily in these two rooms, alongside their European contemporaries.

Barnes was an early advocate for equality in education and provided free seminars in art and philosophy to his majority-Black factory employees, established a scholarship program for Black creators, and was an influential supporter of the Harlem Renaissance. The Foundation continues to honor these values today. Learn more about these initiatives in a small exhibit opposite the gift shop on the lower level.

Temporarily removed
from display

Address 2025 Benjamin Franklin Parkway, Philadelphia, PA 19130, +1 (215) 278-7000, www.barnesfoundation.org | **Getting there** Bus 33 to 20th & Wood Streets | **Hours** Thu–Mon 11am–5pm | **Tip** A short walk from The Barnes, Matthias Baldwin Park is named for 19th-century abolitionist and Black education supporter, whose train factories covered this area for nearly a century (423 N 19th Street, www.baldwinparkphilly.org).

7 — Bartram's Garden

Colonial America's first garden

The Philadelphia Flower Show may be the finest spectacle of modern horticultural prowess in America's "Garden Capital," but the birthplace of the nation is also the birthplace of American gardening. After purchasing 102 riverfront acres in 1728, John Bartram spent the next five decades collecting and nurturing such an astounding assemblage of continental flora that King George III appointed him Royal Botanist for North America. Bartram's exhaustive investigation of colonial plant life brought him international fame and a booming business selling seeds and plants throughout Europe, and he was equally appreciated by American icons like George Washington, who purchased from Bartram for his own Mount Vernon projects.

Today, Bartram's Garden measures "just" 50 acres and is preserved as a free public garden. Come for the natural splendor but spare some time for the collection of original 18th-century buildings onsite, including Bartram's house (ca. 1731) and the Bartram Barn (ca. 1775), believed to be the oldest still-standing barn in Philadelphia County. The medicinal plant display highlights Bartram's contributions to natural healing through his numerous credited discoveries throughout the continent, and the 200-year-old exhibition garden next to the now-landmarked house remains a striking focal point.

But the true stars here reside within the eight-acre historic garden. *Franklinia alatamaha,* a flowering tree that once grew only along the Altamaha River in Georgia, went extinct in the wild by 1803, but not before Bartram collected seeds and successfully cultivated the trees in Pennsylvania, where the species continues to flourish today. Bartram named the beautiful species for his local contemporary of international renown, Ben Franklin. Specimens of this flowering tree in the world today owe their existence to Bartram and his Philadelphia garden.

Address 5400 Lindbergh Boulevard, Philadelphia, PA 19143, +1 (215) 729-5281, www.bartramsgarden.org, info@bartramsgarden.org | **Getting there** Light Rail to S 54th Street & Lindbergh Boulevard (Line 36) | **Hours** Daily dawn–dusk | **Tip** Just a five-minute drive down Elmwood Avenue, Fred's Water Ice serves two dozen flavors of Philly's favorite frozen treat, perfect for an after-garden snack (5343 Chester Avenue, www.fredswaterice.com).

8 Batalá Philly

Philly's most inclusive musical act

When you first learn what Batalá is, it may sound almost prohibitively niche. It's an Afro-Brazilian drum group specifically playing music from Salvador in Bahia, Brazil, and often the work of esteemed founder Giba Gonçalves. The art form incorporates both music and choreography. It takes some stamina, but it turns out to be remarkably accessible. There are chapters around the world, and international groups love to meet up and perform together, and there's no need to speak the same language, even within one's own group. In fact, you don't even need to read music. All Batalá chapters teach their compositions and movements through universal hand signals that allow anyone to learn regardless of language or previous musical experience – and plenty of band members have joined with neither.

In Batalá Philly, President Rosa Barreca confirms you don't need to be a drummer to join the drum band. "What I love most about Batalá is that it finds the drummer in you and brings that person out," she says. Despite the physical demands of performance, members of Batalá Philly have ranged in age from 30–70. They meet twice weekly to rehearse and keep up with a schedule of paid performances that continues to grow with the city's awareness of this fun-loving club.

Batalá is volunteer based, so those performance fees go towards drums, costumes, and operating expenses, as do monthly membership dues. It's a welcoming bunch, as one member describes, "A group in which you can be wholly yourself, and you will be loved and celebrated for it. We are a family, and we lift each other up in drumming and in life."

If you could use a little of that in yourself, then join! If you'd just like to check them out, they rehearse at the Lincoln Monument in Fairmount Park twice weekly, except in winter or inclement weather, when they move indoors. Their website maintains their performance schedule year-round.

Address Kelly & Sedgley Drive, Philadelphia, PA 19130, www.batalaphilly.com, batalaphillylove@gmail.com | Getting there Bus 7, 48, 49 to 29th & Pennsylvania Streets | Hours Seasonally Wed 6–8pm, Sun 11am–1pm | Tip Learn more Afro-Brazilian art forms, like Capoeira, at the ASCAB Capoeira in Center City. All are welcome (1213 Race Street, www.projectcapoeira.com).

9 BioPond

A shockingly secluded secret garden

You won't need a skeleton key or any cryptic passwords to enter this secret garden. On the southwest edge of the University of Pennsylvania campus, the James G. Kaskey Memorial Park, perhaps better known as BioPond, is a small space packed with flora and fauna. Despite its free public admittance, it remains remarkably uncrowded year-round. Though it sits on campus between laboratories and the neighboring hospital complex, even those who work and learn in this bustling zone are often unaware of its existence, leaving it a serene secret hiding in plain sight.

In 1897, this spot was created as a research garden for the university's Biological Department to assist in botanical research and, coincidentally, improve the landscape of the campus. The research garden grew to contain multiple ponds, more than 60 plant rows, and eight greenhouses, with more than 2,000 species available to the department's students and faculty. An expanding campus and even a new street would ultimately chip away at the space over the decades, and today, just around two acres remain. But its heritage as a research garden has left behind a richness rare in urban parks. More than 450 plant species call this small space home, and one pond, the BioPond, remains, with some additional water features enhancing the space.

Come by on any given day, and you're likely to spot plenty of turtles, frogs, and other charming critters enjoying the pond, in addition to the meditative koi swimming within and an abundance of birds throughout. Stretch your legs along the park's modest trails, rest on a bench with a book, or indulge in a picnic at one of the tables. You won't find a ton of signage around the park, but Penn Plant Explorer offers an interactive, zoomable map that identifies many of the plantings, so bring your phone along if you want to know more about the diverse species around you.

Address 433 S University Avenue, Philadelphia, PA 19104, +1 (215) 573-7166,
www.facilities.upenn.edu | Getting there Bus 30, 42, LUCY Green Loop to University
Avenue & VA Medical Center | Hours Daily dawn–dusk | Tip ENIAC, the world's first
computer, was built at UPenn, and some original panels remain within the Moore School
Building. Look for a state historical marker outside the site today (Chancellor Street
between 33rd & 34th Streets, www.phmc.pa.gov).

10 Black Vulture Gallery

Art for your skin, art for your walls

What is art? This age-old question may never have an answer, and Black Vulture Gallery appears to be among the wise who don't even bother to ask. Some passersby are more than a bit confused by the curious storefront, asking themselves, "What is *this*?"

Step inside the high-ceilinged, open space, and you'll be overwhelmed by the sheer volume of framed art, nostalgic vintage, and seemingly random *objets* covering almost every inch of vertical space in the gallery. But head toward the rear, and you'll begin to notice the tattoo stations of Black Vulture's own artists. Stop in on the weekend, usually Saturdays, and you're likely to find the space hosting local bands, too. Whether your preferred art is painted, stitched, inked, or played, you'll find it in this funky Fishtown gallery of all things art.

Black Vulture's diverse artists claim to be able to handle any custom commission, and, after more than ten years in business and scores of rave reviews from repeat customers, their track record appears to back up the claim. Despite the range in artistic talents offered here, there's a clear focus on the precision blackout tattoos for which the gallery and its owner, Hoode, have become particularly renowned. But even if you're not down for something quite so bold, you'll find what you're looking for here whether you know what that is yet or not.

These sought-after artists are busy, but the friendly, energetic vibe of the studio is far more collaborative than intimidating. Walk-ins are possible when available, though hours aren't firm, and artists tend to be well booked. So call ahead and make a reservation if you're serious about acquiring some new body art and don't want to leave empty-armed. Still, you can pop in just to browse the walls during gallery shows or otherwise. There's always plenty to see and hear here, whether you're in the market for ink or not.

Address 208 E Girard Avenue, Philadelphia, PA 19125, +1 (215) 423-3666, www.blackvulturegallery.com, blackvulturegallery@yahoo.com | **Getting there** Light Rail to Girard & Frankford Avenues (Line 15); Bus 5, 25 to Frankford & Girard Avenues | **Hours** See website | **Tip** Three blocks west, Rocky's Crystals & Minerals offers additional eye-candy for magpie shoppers drawn to the shiny and curious (310 E Girard Avenue, www.rockyscrystalsonline.com).

11_BOK

Vintage cheese, anyone?

What was once the Bok Vocational High School was originally built in 1936 as a hulking technical facility teaching disciplines from wallpapering to cosmetology to 3,000 Philadelphia students in need of a trade. It is now simply BOK, a *very* mixed-use space with highly specialized spaces for rent, and home to a population as diverse as ever, though it has traded students for professionals (mostly).

The development firm Scout purchased the building at auction from the city school district in 2013. They left the historic exterior intact and took an intentionally "light-touch approach" to the interior, preserving the building's unique features and capabilities to match them with tenants ideally suited to their functions. Today, the 340,000-square-foot space hosts more than 250 businesses and, despite popular belief, they're not all creatives. Much of the space is designed for more artistic and technical endeavors, and those fields do comprise the majority of tenants. But you'll also find the likes of chiropractors, skin care specialists, and marketing consultants within. It's often a first office / first studio for entrepreneurs making their way from sofa to home office to public-facing space, and that has included everyone from piano tuners and vintage cheese mongers to textile recyclers and a Cambodian performing arts organization.

Come in for free weekly tours on Wednesdays, or explore on your own, browsing from a handful of shops and open studios among the bunch. Or head straight to the rooftop café, one of several eateries and bakeries at BOK, if you fancy a bite and a view. Year-round BOK hosts community events, including plant swamps, candlelight concerts, and film festivals, so there's always an excuse to pop in if you're the type who needs a mission too. This place is welcoming and inspiring for all; you'll find your reason to love it no matter who you are.

Address 1901 S 9th Street, Philadelphia, PA 19148, +1 (215) 419-5121, www.buildingbok.com, hello@buildingbok.com | **Getting there** Bus 47M to 9th & Mifflin Streets, or 47 to 8th & Mifflin Streets | **Hours** Daily 10am–5pm | **Tip** If you need a rest after exploring BOK, the well-maintained and peaceful Dickinson Square Park is not far (1600 E Moyamensing Avenue, https://dswca.org).

12　Buist Sophora

A beloved tree that defies destruction

It may sound more like a magical spell than anything else, but Buist Sophora is one of many names given to the tree standing opposite the northeast corner of Buist Park in the Elmwood Park neighborhood. It's been here at least 100 years despite multiple threats, so perhaps it holds some magic after all.

Robert Buist was once one of the country's most respected and financially successful horticulturists after emigrating from Scotland and opening his nursery in 1850 right near where the tree stands today. We don't know exactly when this specimen of Sophora tree was planted, potentially by Buist himself, but we can be reasonably sure it was already here in 1919 when it appears to have been described as the largest in the entire Philadelphia region. At this time, it was in danger from the ax, as the new General Electric plant brought a need for dense housing in the area. But it was somehow spared, out-lived the factory's 60-year-existence entirely, and remains today in a neighborhood that's more crowded than ever. Not only is the tree still here, but the lot next to it remains respectfully empty, and the neighborhood has sacrificed coveted street parking space in favor of this behemoth's greedy root system.

The Sophora goes by other names, including the Chinese Scholar and the Japanese Pagoda, though it's actually not native to Japan at all (this name comes from its association with Buddhist temples) and is, as you might now guess, not native to the northeastern United States either. They're extremely adaptable to a variety of soil conditions, though, and they also provide tremendous shade. Best of all, they hold their leaves until late fall, after an explosive flowering season in late summer.

Not much remains today of the once renowned Robert Buist or his son, who died "the millionaire seedsman," except for this persistent tree and the neighboring park named for them.

Address Hobson Street between Buist and Elmwood Avenues, Philadelphia, PA 19142 |
Getting there Light Rail to Elmwood Avenue & 68th Street (Line 36) | Hours
Unrestricted | Tip The NASA Moon Tree was once the city's coolest tree, having grown
from a seed that went to the moon and back. It's gone now, but a plaque remains where it
once stood in Washington Square (632 Walnut Street, www.nasa.gov).

13 Burlesque Academy

Get your Gypsy Rose Lee on

Burlesque wasn't always a strip-tease art, but it was never tame. Initially a British discipline, the earliest burlesque performances were often risqué parodies of popular operas, characterized by humor and exaggeration. It was the Americans who introduced the fine art of sensual clothes-shedding to the spectacle when it took hold here in the mid 19th century, and Philadelphia was prime burlesque territory.

Concentrated slightly north of Center City, Philly's small vice district, the now-vanished Tenderloin, was home to around a dozen burlesque theaters. The star of these was the Arch Street Opera House, later known as the Trocadero Theater, which continued entertaining the city until its unfortunate closing in 2019. It's here that Gypsy Rose Lee was discovered by Billy Minsky and became the international superstar still most associated with the art today. Though American burlesque began with a multi-gender, multi-race openness, it had already shifted to a predominantly white male audience by the time Lee took the country by storm, but a resurgence of the art in the late 20th century has since sought to return the discipline to its inclusive roots, especially in Philadelphia.

The Philadelphia Burlesque Academy has an "all bodies, genders, races, abilities, and ages (18+)" inclusion policy in its environment of respect that welcomes everyone to this uniquely expressive art. And there's a seriously impressive menu of classes to choose from. If you're casually curious, consider a first-timer lesson, or perhaps even drop in for a stocking peel class, where you'll spend the entire lesson honing your technique for this particular skill. Whether your interests lie in lap dancing, chair tease, twerking, or full-on professional act development, owners Ginger Leigh and Cherry Bomb, along with their skilled team of instructors, are ready to welcome and encourage you.

Address 2101 E Huntingdon Street, Unit 1, Philadelphia, PA 19125, +1 (215) 298-9860,
www.philadelphiaburlesqueacademy.com, contact@philadelphiaburlesqueacademy.com |
Getting there Bus 5, 39 to Huntingdon Street & Frankford Avenue | Hours See website for
class schedule | Tip Franky Bradley's hosts a monthly burlesque show by La Maison Rose
for those times you'd rather just watch (1320 Chancellor Street, www.frankybradleys.com).

14 __ Carmen's

Where Obama went for a cheesesteak

One of the quickest ways to start a fight among pretty much anyone in Philadelphia is to ask where to find the best cheesesteak in the city. While everyone in and around Philly is positive that no other city in the world can make a Philly cheesesteak properly (no matter what ridiculous claims their signs make) almost no one can agree on who *in* the city does it best. Whether it's the quality of the roll, the type of cheese, or the ratio of beef to bread, there seem to be enough ways of varying the simple sandwich to cause widespread disagreement on the top recipe.

Even visitors know of the iconic rivalry between Pat's and Geno's, sitting opposite each other at the crossroads of Passyunk Avenue and 9th Street. Most tourists agonize over which to try when in town (both, obviously), but one high-profile out-of-towner made national news when he bypassed both for Carmen's Famous Italian Hoagies & Cheesesteaks in Reading Terminal Market.

In 2010, then-President Barack Obama grabbed two cheesesteaks to go during an unplanned stop at the world-famous indoor marketplace by the Pennsylvania Convention Center, putting Carmen's in the national spotlight. It wasn't actually the president's restaurant choice that was headline worthy, but the simple fact that he ordered correctly. In 2004, presidential hopeful John Kerry ordered a cheesesteak with Swiss cheese, deeply wounding countless Philadelphians who would only ever approve of Cheez Whiz, and giving his opposition ammo to dub him "out of touch" with the working classes. Obama ordered correctly and won re-election in 2012. Coincidence? We'll never know.

We won't say a cheesesteak lost the election for Kerry, but we can't say it didn't, either. Pop in to Carmen's to try a presidential cheesesteak for yourself. If you want to order exactly like him, ask for sweet peppers and mushrooms. With Cheez Whiz, of course.

Address 51 N 12th Street, Philadelphia, PA 19107, +1 (215) 592-7799, www.readingterminalmarket.org | **Getting there** Subway to 11th Street (Market–Frankford Line); Bus 23, 48 to Arch & 12th Streets | **Hours** Daily 8am–6pm | **Tip** To try Philly's other favorite sandwich, grab a roast pork and broccoli rabe at Tommy DiNic's, also in RTM. It was crowned the winner of Adam Richman's *The Best Sandwich in America* during the show's 2012 finale (51 N 12th Street, www.readingterminalmarket.org).

15 ___ Cave of Kelpius

Where America's first mystic cult awaited Doomsday

Philadelphia may be best known for its revolutionary history, but there's a fascinating bit of 17th-century history in the hills of Wissahickon Valley Park. Also known as Hermit's Cave, the Cave of Kelpius is traditionally believed to be the site where a young Johannes Kelpius brought the Rosicrucian Order to the Americas in 1694 and tucked himself away to await the end days with his brotherhood of 40 monks.

Needless to say, Armageddon did not come, but the brotherhood remained at the cave until at least 1708, when Kelpius died at the age of 41 and the group's fervor fizzled out. During the cult's 12 years at this site, they practiced a mysticism deeply rooted in numerology and astrology and claimed to have ancient wisdom dating to early Egypt. The Hermits of the Wissahickon, as locals called them, were neither shunned by other area settlers nor completely left to a hermetic lifestyle but rather consulted for their deep knowledge of medicine and admired for their musical talents. The order, when not spending time in solitary meditation in the woods, even operated a school for Germantown children in a large meetinghouse they constructed.

The "Society of the Woman in the Wilderness," as Kelpius dubbed his brotherhood, was all male, despite the potentially misleading name. The woman referenced here is not a society member, but an apocalyptic figure from the *Book of Revelation*. Among other legends surrounding Kelpius, some believed he was in possession of the immortality-granting philosopher's stone (which you may now associate with *Harry Potter*) and voluntarily tossed it in the Wissahickon River the year before his death.

There's no doubt Kelpius lived in these woods. Some people claim the cave is merely an old spring house, but archaeological evidence shows otherwise, and the state has seen fit to honor the spot with a historical marker.

Address 777 Hermit Lane, Philadelphia, PA 19128, +1 (215) 247-0417, www.fow.org |
Getting there By car, take I-76 W to Exit 340A. Hermit Lane is at the southern end of
Wissahickon Valley Park, then walk the Yellow trail. | Hours Apr–Nov, daily 6–1am,
Dec–Mar, daily 6am–8pm | Tip For a beautiful view of the woods surrounding Hermit's
Cave, take a short walk west and climb to Lover's Leap. The views of the gorge are beautiful
from here, and the best access point is from Hermit Lane, where you're already parked.

16 Charles Dickens' Desk

Not his only, but his last

Charles Dickens was a 19th-century British writer, who indeed spent his entire life living in England. But the possessions of the famous are often scattered, especially when auctions come into play, and that's precisely how the renowned author's desk has come to rest in the Rare Book Room of the Free Library of Philadelphia (see ch. 4). But don't fret – there's plenty of connection between Dickens and Philadelphia, both physically and thematically.

Already famous during his lifetime, Dickens made two trips to Philadelphia, 26 years apart. After the first in 1842, he left somewhat lackluster reviews of the city's too-regular street grid in his diary and lamented that some of the sights were dreary, but he was heartily impressed by both Pennsylvania Hospital and the Water Works. Most interestingly, though, he met with then-resident Edgar Allan Poe (see ch. 31), who was not nearly as famous as Dickens and would never be during his own lifetime. Dickens spent most of his free time investigating Eastern State Penitentiary, particularly the solitary confinement practice he found barbaric (this would later influence scenes in *A Tale of Two Cities*). He returned a quarter century later in 1868, even more famous, and again stopped in Philadelphia during his American reading tour. While he may not have gushed over Philly's intrigue, the working-class struggle of the city is one all too familiar to many Dickensian characters and settings, so it's safe to say he certainly understood Philadelphia, if not delighting in it.

Sold at auction after his death, Dickens' final desk, one he used for more than three decades and on which he was penning *The Mystery of Edwin Drood* when he suddenly died, now sits permanently on display at the Free Library. Turning back to the Dickens / Poe bromance for a moment, the library is also home to Dickens' stuffed pet raven, Grip, who inspired Poe's poem "The Raven."

Address 1901 Vine Street, 3rd Floor, Philadelphia, PA 19103, +1 (215) 825-5357, www.freelibrary.org | Getting there Bus 33 to 20th & Wood Streets | Hours Mon–Fri 9am–5pm | Tip One of only two Dickens sculptures in the world is located at Clark Park in Philadelphia. Dickens requested none ever be made, but this one depicts him with character Little Nell of *The Old Curiosity Shop* (4300 Baltimore Avenue, www.friendsofclarkpark.org).

17 Cherry Street Pier

An abandoned space turned community inspiration

Just beyond the Benjamin Franklin Bridge, Municipal Pier 9 was once the largest pier in Philadelphia. When the city set out to revive its industrial waterfront in the early 20th century, a plan that also included building that beautiful bridge above, the 535-foot by 100-foot pier was a vital transition between cargo ships on the Delaware River and the major railroads leaving Philadelphia. Business boomed until the middle of the century.

Today, few piers of this project remain, and Pier 9 is the only one to retain towering remnants of its original head house. Abandoned for decades, it was renamed Cherry Street Pier and opened as mixed-use public space in 2018, now with a sensibility veering decidedly more artistic than industrial.

The indoor-outdoor pier is now home to glass-front artist studios inside recycled shipping containers, an exhibition gallery, an expansive marketplace showcasing the works of local artists and makers, a performance and lecture venue, and an open-air garden on the water (more of a public gathering place than a traditional "garden"). In the evenings, restaurant vendors operate out of repurposed historic trolley cars in a unique take on the food truck scene, and there is, of course, a bar, too.

Cherry Street Pier is open every day and is free to the public, but keep an eye out for regular events, like the summer weekend farmers market and monthly First Friday festivities. Cultural markets, art exhibitions, flea markets, vintage fairs, and all manner of bazaars make their way through the pier's annual calendar, too, so there's always something new to find here no matter how often you visit. If you're a remote worker, this is also a great spot for you to snag a table and bang out a few hours of productivity with free WiFi and an upgraded view. All told, there are 64,000 square feet of space waiting to inspire you here.

Address 121 N Columbus Boulevard, Philadelphia, PA 19106, +1 (215) 923-0818, www.cherrystreetpier.com, cherrystreetpier@drwc.org | Getting there Bus 25 to Columbus Boulevard & Race Street | Hours Mon–Thu noon–10pm, Fri noon–11pm, Sat 11am–11pm, Sun 11am–10pm | Tip For even more dramatic views and a quieter scene, neighboring Race Street Pier, even closer to the bridge, offers space for strolls and sit-downs on the promenade and lawn (Race Street & Columbus Boulevard, www.delawareriverwaterfront.org).

18　Cherry Street Tavern

Is that a urinal trough along the bar?

If you're looking for the wildest bathroom setup in Philadelphia, local lore might send you straight to the Cherry Street Tavern. There's nothing particularly unusual about the tavern's actual restroom, but take a seat at the bar and you'll discover its most curious feature: a trough runs the length of the floor along the counter. The tavern dates to 1905 and survived Prohibition by doubling as a barbershop-with-a-twist, but most of its early history as a working-class watering hole is lost to the ages, leaving plenty of room for that famous Philly imagination.

Legend has long held that the bar trough was a urinal. Local media has gone as far as to publish that patrons could once eat, drink, and urinate here without getting up. But this story was never quite true. That isn't to say that no patrons ever did urinate in the trough, but there's another reason this trifecta of human comfort never occurred simultaneously, and it's more a matter of timeline.

The trough is a remnant of pre-Prohibition life, when chewing tobacco was the norm for the average blue-collar laborer. Constant chewing brings constant and excessive spitting and, while any expectorating is generally considered unpleasant today, the spit formed while chewing tobacco has always been particularly unappreciated. The already unsavory taverns of yesteryear would install flow trough spittoons along the base of the bar, and water would carry away the unwanted byproduct.

While the troughs were never intended to be urinals, historians say it's not only possible, but likely, that they were occasionally used by lazy patrons spying an easy opportunity for relief without stepping away from the bar. So why is it unlikely anyone ever ate, drank, and urinated from one seat here? The tavern didn't start serving its now famous roast beef sandwiches or any other food until the 1970s, when the trough had long been out of service.

Address 129 N 22nd Street, Philadelphia, PA 19103, +1 (215) 561-5683,
www.cherrysttavern.com | Getting there Bus 7, 48 to 22nd & Race Streets | Hours
Tue–Thu 11:30am–11pm, Fri & Sat 11:30am–1am | Tip On a nice day, consider bringing
your roast beef sandwich to Coxe Park, a quaint pocket park halfway down the block, perfect
for a sit-down after a pint at the tavern (2134 Cherry Street, www.friendsofcoxepark.com).

19__Cira Green

A complete park in the sky

Like most of America's largest cities, Philadelphia is predominantly developed, so there isn't much hope for more green space to find its way to the city's streets. But that doesn't mean new parks are out of the question entirely. Atop Cira Centre South, engineering innovations bring not just another green roof to Philly, but an entire park (just over an acre) that also includes blue roof engineering to keep more than 700,000 gallons of rainwater out of the city's storm sewers annually. It's a blue-green roof, but you don't even need to understand what's happening under your feet to enjoy this 12th-story escape in University City.

Graced with several spacious lawns, including a sloped amphitheater lawn that offers extra special views, the space is open to the public daily and has plenty of fun features for general use. It's also home to the city's largest outdoor screen, which is perfect for special events, from Kentucky Derby parties to costumed video game tournaments (and yes, you can reserve it for your own private events, too).

On a more regular basis, look out for weekly rooftop block parties, golden hour cornhole showdowns, and Saturday morning cartoon picnics. Come hungry, regardless of your reason for visiting, because the Sunset Social snack bar offers a sizable selection of burgers, sandwiches, and bowls, alongside drinks, both alcoholic and otherwise. Oh, and even though the "really long hot dog" is on the kids' menu, it's pretty popular with adults, too, so don't be too shy to order it. You can also bring your own food for a picnic, but no outside alcohol is permitted.

Cira Green is open year-round, and, while you may be more inclined to visit an open-air rooftop park in summer, there's at least one serious advantage to ascending the tower in cooler weather. It's the only time of year you can get into the park for humbling sunrise views.

Address 129 S 30th Street, Philadelphia, PA 19104, +1 (267) 295-9565, www.ciragreen.com, ciragreeninfo@bdnreit.com | **Getting there** Subway to 30th Street (Market–Frankford Line); Light Rail to 30th Street (Line 10); Bus 21, 42 to Chestnut & 30th Streets | **Hours** Sun–Tue 7am–9pm, Wed–Sat 7am–10pm | **Tip** The city's largest green roof is at the PECO headquarters, and you can visit it through monthly tours led by the Pennsylvania Horticultural Society (2301 Market Street, www.phsonline.org).

20 Circadium School of Contemporary Circus

The first state-accredited program for circus arts

Forget about running away to join the circus – it's not that easy anymore! Philadelphia's Circadium School of Contemporary Circus turns the notion of clown school on its head with the country's first state-accredited higher education program in circus arts. The three-year program encompasses everything from acrobatics and aerial skills to financial management and marketing to help carry the next generation of circus artists into the future. But you don't need to enroll to enjoy the fun.

One Thursday per month, Circadium welcomes the public with Test Flights. Like an open mic for performers, Test Flights opens the campus' Sanctuary to artists looking to dry-run their acts in front of live audiences in a supportive environment. The acts run the gamut from circus and theater to dance and spoken word. If you're an artist interested in participating, it's as easy as applying online and showing up. But if you're not the steal-the-spotlight sort and just want to take in some daring acts from across performance genres, sitting in the audience is free. You'll also find occasional ticketed events performed by students.

If you've had some intermediate circus arts experience and want to kick it up a notch without devoting the next three years of your life to a full-time program, Circadium has launched a one-week intensive program that mimics the three-year curriculum in a crash course – decidedly not for beginners. There are occasional skill-specific workshops for all skill levels open to the public if you're just looking to dip your toes into this fascinating world. But if you're simply an admirer of the circus arts or have only dabbled, stick to the audience during Test Flights and revel in free monthly performances right in your own backyard.

Address 6452 Greene Street, Philadelphia, PA 19119, +1 (215) 849-1991, www.circadium.com, info@circadium.com | **Getting there** Train to Upsal (Chestnut Hill West Line); Bus H to Johnson & Greene Streets | **Hours** See website for schedule | **Tip** The completely inexperienced can clown around at sister school Philadelphia School of Circus Arts at the same address (6452 Greene Street, www.phillycircus.com).

21 The Clay Studio
Learn, create, and "clay it forward"

The Clay Studio is no small workshop for a handful of quiet artists. It may have started that way in 1974, when a teacher and several students pooled resources to support each other's work, but it was only a matter of a few years before the studio shifted its focus outward to community education, becoming a non-profit in 1979.

In 2021, The Clay Studio moved to its new home. Its 34,000-square-foot space is, itself, a work of art in South Kensington, a residential community where Director of Artist Programs Jennifer Zwilling says the studio can better serve neighborhood families, as it now sits within walking distance of many homes and schools. The new space also hosts an afterschool program for area students to hang out, do homework, and get creative. And for those schools and groups unable to reach the studio, The Clay Studio launched the Claymobile to bridge the gap itself, annually reaching 4,000+ Philadelphians who would otherwise miss out.

Students are not the only focus of The Clay Studio, though. In fact, the socially-minded missions of the studio include everyone, regardless of skill, background, or financial position. Diversity and inclusion are the core of the studio's ethos, and three-tier class pricing means no one is turned away; there's a standard price, a community-supported price, and a "clay it forward" option to include a little extra toward another's class fees. There's also a free weekly workshop on Saturdays.

The new space is home to a 700-piece gallery of works by former guest and resident artists. Don't miss the eclectic shop, the star of which is the memorable Cup Wall. Featuring more than 200 handmade mugs of every possible form, decoration, glaze, and size, the wall isn't just a shoppable showroom for customers, it's an interactive encyclopedia for the studio's roughly 500 students, and it highlights the fact that creativity has no limits.

Address 1425 N American Street, Philadelphia, PA 19122, +1 (215) 925-3453, www.theclaystudio.org, info@theclaystudio.org | Getting there Bus 57 to American & Master Streets | Hours Mon–Fri 11am–6pm, Sat & Sun 11am–5pm | Tip Across the street, Crane Arts is home to many studios and galleries, most of which are open to the public on Saturdays and the second Thursday of each month (1400 N American Street, www.cranearts.com).

22 The Colored Girls Museum

A curated collection in a private home

In a three-story, Germantown Victorian, Vashti Dubois curates a collection of objects specific to the life, history, and experience of the colored girl. The Colored Girls Museum chose its name not just to honor the black and brown skin tones of its namesake subjects, but to illustrate the ways in which the girls and women of the African Diaspora have been colored by outsiders with labels like "too loud" or "too angry," and the expectations and alterations these terms force upon them. Presented as a self-described "memoir museum," the collection includes art, artifacts, and memorabilia in exhibits that expose both triumphs and tragedies, aiming not just to educate and celebrate, but to serve as a research facility and think tank for the future of this historically misrepresented group.

The museum started as a temporary exhibition during the city's Fringe Arts Festival before becoming permanent in 2015. The decision to maintain the collection in a lived-in house parallels the museum's mission to spotlight the ordinary girl. Here, it's not about celebrities or well-known historical figures, but the everyday girl and her real-world experience, at whichever time she lived or lives. While the focus rests solidly on the female experience, one room, belonging to Dubois' son, does explore The Colored Boy.

Evolving exhibits take up much of the museum's space, so specific pieces may be adapted, repurposed, or replaced between your visits. You'll find everything from painting and photography to historical fashion, furniture, and everyday objects of cultural significance.

In addition to offering salon-style tours for groups of 10 or more, the museum hosts special events and has been partially funded by the likes of the Knight Foundation and the Greater Philadelphia Cultural Alliance, among other notable organizations.

Address 4613 Newhall Street, Philadelphia, PA 19144, +1 (267) 630-4438, www.thecoloredgirlsmuseum.com, thecoloredgirlsmuseum@gmail.com | Getting there Bus 53 to Wayne Avenue & Apsley Street | Hours Sat & Sun by appointment only | Tip The Paul Robeson House is another Black female-led house museum in Philadelphia that should be visited and explored (4951 Walnut Street, www.paulrobesonhouse.org).

23 — Congress Hall
Move over, Independence Hall

If you grew up in the Philadelphia area, you certainly took at least one class trip to Independence Hall to gaze upon the Assembly Room, where both the Declaration of Independence and the United States Constitution were signed. And even if you're a transplant who's only ever played tourist in your new home city once or twice, this destination was most likely on your itinerary. It's well worth a visit, certainly, but the adjoining building on the corner of Chestnut and 6th Streets has even more to ogle and consider.

Sure, it's essentially impossible to top the historical importance of both the Declaration *and* the Constitution, but neighboring Congress Hall is where many of the developments following these signings occurred, including the inaugurations of both Washington and Adams, the ratification of the Bill of Rights, and the creation of the United States Navy. Originally constructed as the Philadelphia County Courthouse in 1787, it was quickly expanded and repurposed to accommodate Congress for the 10 year period in which Philly served as the nation's temporary capital, beginning in 1790.

The House of Representatives met on the first floor of Congress Hall, while the Senate convened on the slightly posher second floor. Among the contents are 28 original desks, where the Founding Fathers mapped out the new country's path. And look for an impressive pair of portraits hanging in second-floor committee rooms. You may recognize them as France's King Louis XVI and Queen Marie Antoinette, who provided financial and military support to the Americans and gifted the art to the newly-formed nation after the successful Revolution. Also on display is an early document bearing a banded red ink stain illustrating the 18th-century practice of binding official documents in red tape, giving rise to the notion of bureaucratic "red tape" that persists today.

Address Chestnut Street & 6th Street, Philadelphia, PA 19106, +1 (215) 965-2305, www.nps.gov | **Getting there** Subway to 5th Street/Independence Hall (Market–Frankford Line) | **Hours** Daily 9am–5pm | **Tip** One block from Congress Hall, you'll find the ruins of the first executive mansion, used by Washington and Adams during this period and now devoted to acknowledging the country's hypocritical history with slavery (Market Street & 6th Street, www.nps.gov).

24 Curtis Institute

Free education and free concerts

There may be no such thing as a free lunch, but there are plenty of other freebies in Philadelphia – and some of them are otherwise much more expensive than a simple meal. Considering the soaring costs of higher education nationwide, it's astounding to recognize that Philadelphia's Curtis Institute of Music is a tuition-free institution offering both undergrad and graduate degrees to talented students.

Understandably, it's not easy to gain admittance to Curtis, whose reputational peers include Juilliard and the Boston Conservatory. The school's acceptance rate hovers around an ultra-competitive 5%, and even successful applicants must still audition live for final confirmation. While it's fabulous to know that Philadelphia offers such an astonishing education at no cost to its musical protégés, this is more than just a fun fact to stick under your cap – all Philadelphians (and savvy visitors) can benefit from having this venerable institution in our backyard.

As you might hope, this concentrated collection of musically-gifted students provides the institute with enough superior talent to form its own symphony orchestra and opera, each offering an annual calendar of professional-quality performances. If you have young ones in tow, drop into the family concert series, where they can begin to build an appreciation for classical music with attention-level appropriate, interactive programs geared toward ages 5-12.

Perhaps most appealing and certainly most universally accessible, students of the Curtis Institute offer free weekly concerts throughout the academic season as they hone their skills on the way to becoming tomorrow's headliners. These performances come at no cost, but they do still require reservations. If you can't snag a ticket, you can still enjoy the performances live streaming on the Curtis Institute's Facebook page or YouTube channel.

Address 1726 Locust Street, Philadelphia, PA 19103, +1 (215) 893-5252, www.curtis.edu, tickets@curtis.edu | **Getting there** Bus 12 to Locust & 17th Streets | **Hours** See website for performance schedule | **Tip** The Philadelphia Art Alliance offers exhibits and workshops across artistic disciplines just one block away (251 S 18th Street, www.philartalliance.org).

25 DeLong Building
A stunning model of urban fire history

Philadelphia isn't just home to the country's first fire company; it was also the first municipality in the United States to pass a fire escape law in 1876. In response to some well-reported factory fires, Philly leaders felt it was time to add some life-saving protection to its larger buildings and created a board that could mandate any structure to include a fire escape. The state followed suit three years later.

Unfortunately, there were few guidelines provided and almost no enforcement of these laws locally within a few years, so the board was disbanded, and few buildings complied with what essentially became a vague suggestion. The state amended its law in 1885 to specify the construction of external, iron fire escapes, and it wasn't long after this that the DeLong Building was constructed. It remains today as a gorgeous reply to the law many considered a hideous blight on urban architecture.

Built in 1899, the seven-story brick DeLong Building is beloved by architecture appreciators for many of the qualities that make it an exemplar of the Chicago School (also known as "commercial style"), but absolutely anyone can appreciate its magnificent fire escape. The building's architects (who remain a subject of debate today) were likely as daunted as the majority of the day's designers who were mandated to include external fire escapes, considered by many to be scars on otherwise beautiful buildings. Their response, though, was a mesmerizingly ornate wrought-iron escape that remains the building's artistic focal point today.

Remarkably, this stunner didn't make its way to the Philadelphia Register of Historic Places until 2022, but it's now preserved and protected. Come by to consider Philly's rich role in fire-fighting history as you ogle the beauty of the DeLong. If you really love it, you can even live inside the former office building today. It's a desirable address, but units do come on the market for sale or rent from time to time.

Address 1232 Chestnut Street, Philadelphia, PA 19107 | Getting there Bus 9, 21, 42 to Chestnut & 13th Streets | Hours Unrestricted | Tip There's much more Philly fire history to learn at the Fireman's Hall Museum, a 10-minute drive from the DeLong Building (147 N 2nd Street, www.firemanshallmuseum.org).

26 Dirty Franks

Eye-popping dive with serious heart

There's a lot to see inside this corner bar at Pine and 13th Streets, but one thing is conspicuously missing from the exterior: a sign. You'll have to know what you're looking for when visiting Dirty Franks, but it's not difficult. There may be no words advertising the business, but there are plenty of famous Franks painted on the exterior, ranging from Frank Sinatra and Frank Lloyd Wright to Aretha *Frank*lin and *Frank*enstein. Even Pope Francis was added in 2015, the year of his visit to the city.

Inside, the spectacle continues with a bar covered in photographs of patrons, parties, and all manner of Dirty Franks history from its 90+ years serving the neighborhood. Look up and you'll find paper snowflakes (yes, the kind you made in elementary school) dangling from the ceiling tiles. These are made by locals too, and you can likely contribute one if you're the crafty sort. Some walls serve as a local art gallery, hawking a curious array of pieces at a range of price points, while others display dislodged hubcaps from unfortunate driversby, a Hall of Fame advertising annual winners of the Customer of the Year award, and a memorial wall for Dirty Franks family who've passed. (The wife of one now-deceased patron dumped his ashes in a hole in the wall near the dartboard, so avoid that area if you're superstitious!)

Legend has it that Bob Dylan was once thrown out of Dirty Franks, but, like much of the bar's legendary history, it's tough to back this one up. Just about no one else is kicked out of this haven for the offbeat though. So come by for conversation and the guaranteed opportunity to get to know neighborhood locals who could quickly become like family. The Dirty Franks community is strong and welcoming, provided you don't spend your visit staring at your phone. This is a place to bring your own stories and come away with plenty of new ones.

Address 347 S 13th Street, Philadelphia, PA 19107, +1 (215) 732-5010, www.facebook.com/
dirtyfranksbar, info@dirtyfranksbar.com | Getting there Subway to Lombard–South
(Broad Street Line); Bus 40 to Pine & 13th Streets | Hours Wed–Sun 1pm–2am, Mon
& Tue 4pm–2am | Tip A few doors down on the corner of 13th and Panama Streets,
Sweet Box Bakeshop serves 16 daily flavors of decadent cupcakes (339 S 13th Street,
www.shopsweetbox.com).

27 Discovery Center

From forgotten reservoir to city treasure

The East Park Reservoir was the primary provider of Philadelphia's drinking water for almost 80 years, but all good things must come to an end. The 37-acre reservoir was abandoned in 1970, and a new border fence kept Strawberry Mansion neighborhood recreationalists out. The area developed into a haven for migratory birds traveling the Atlantic Flyway, and the deserted West Basin evolved into an unspoiled lake surrounded by lush vegetation, welcoming more than 130 identified bird species.

In the fall of 2018, humans were finally welcomed back, but not at the expense of the birds. On the contrary, the point was to appreciate the birds and the unique wildlife surrounding the reservoir with the opening of the multi-million-dollar Discovery Center.

Philadelphia's Discovery Center marks the nation's first ever partnership between The Audubon Society and Outward Bound, who joined forces to realize this environmental education endeavor that protects this special habitat. The center is also home to Outward Bound Philadelphia, which uses nature programs to challenge people of all ages through character-building itineraries and is especially regarded for its success with at-risk youth and young adults.

The Discovery Center has reopened this gorgeous natural environment to Philadelphia residents and visitors looking for an exquisite escape from daily life. The center and its regular programming are also free to the public and open six days per week. Beyond the Visitor Center, with its pollinator garden, water walk, and education exhibits, The Discovery Center packs its calendar with events, from photography hikes to canoeing and conservation days – and hosting game nights and birding clubs between, all while Audubon Mid-Atlantic conducts its conservation research and Outward Bound continues its community outreach from this unexpected oasis in Fairmount Park.

Address 3401 Reservoir Drive, Philadelphia, PA 19121, +1 (610) 990-3431, www.discoveryphila.org | Getting there Bus 3 to Reservoir & Smith Day Nursery Drives | Hours See website for seasonal hours and programs | Tip For conservation and birding at a more grassroots level, check out the nearly hidden Spruce Hill Bird Sanctuary, 15 minutes southwest of here by car (233 S Melville Street, www.sprucehillca.org).

28 Dream Garden

A masterpiece nearly lost

Designed by Maxfield Parrish and created by Louis Comfort Tiffany, Philadelphia's *Dream Garden* was a renowned masterpiece when first installed at the Curtis Publishing Building over a century ago. More than 100,000 glass tiles, hand-fired to achieve a staggering 260 colors, comprise the epic mural that spans 15 by 49 feet, and the dazzling piece even had a buzzy New York preview before its six-month installation in the Philadelphia lobby.

Over time, the *Dream Garden* garnered considerably less attention and caught the gaze of few eyes beyond those entering the lobby for routine business, leaving the potentially priceless mural languishing in a fog of distant memory – until someone wanted it.

In 1998, soon-to-be billionaire hotelier Steve Wynn took a liking to the *Dream Garden* and thought it would find better exposure at one of his casinos in Las Vegas, where he sought to relocate the enormous piece. Wynn initiated the purchase of the piece, but Philadelphians took poorly to the news, despite virtually ignoring the work for decades. Two friends formed the Arts Defense League with the sole purpose of stopping the move, collecting signatures daily in front of the Curtis Building and eventually catching the attention of national media, including *People* magazine. As protests mounted, Wynn ultimately backed out of the sale. The Pew Charitable Trusts purchased the piece through a $3.5 million grant, gifting ownership to the Pennsylvania Academy of Fine Arts (see ch. 48).

Dream Garden remains in its original location, now known as the Curtis Center, as a once-again prized Philadelphia possession thanks, primarily, to one man's desire to take it away. In fact, Philadelphia became so concerned with losing something it cared little about that the Philadelphia Historical Commission created the category "historical object" for the mural, so it will never face threat of removal again.

Address 601 Walnut Street, Philadelphia, PA 19106, +1 (215) 238-6450, www.associationforpublicart.org, apa@associationforpublicart.org | **Getting there** Subway to 5th Street/Independence Hall (Market–Frankford Line); Bus 9, 21, 42 to Walnut & 7th Streets | **Hours** Mon–Fri 8am–6pm, Sat 10am–1pm | **Tip** A two-minute walk south, the Athenaeum of Philadelphia exhibits antiquities and arts in a striking Italianate Revival style building (219 S 6th Street, www.philaathenaeum.org).

29 Earliest US Serial Killer

The devil in the white city met his end in Philadelphia

He may not have been the first serial killer in world history, but H. H. Holmes was the first in the United States. Best known today as "the devil in the white city," thanks to the best-selling novel of the same name by Erik Larson, Holmes's reputation comes from his time spent in Chicago. But it's here in Philadelphia where he met his dramatic end.

On the surface, Holmes appeared to earn his living in Chicago as a pharmacist. He actually built most of his wealth through murder and insurance scams, and life insurance was his bread and butter. The fraudulent doctor's employees were required to list him as their beneficiary, and he routinely collected after murdering them. But this was nothing compared to what he would achieve during the World's Columbian Exposition of 1893. The centerpiece of his operation was his intricately built "murder castle" hotel, containing plenty of secret passageways, trap doors, and soundproof rooms, plus a gas chamber and a crematorium. Throughout the Expo, Holmes preyed on starry-eyed women visiting the dazzling exhibits, eventually seducing them into marriage engagements before bumping them off to secure their assets. When he didn't cremate his victims, he sold the bodies to medical schools for a bit of extra pocket change.

The historical marker here tells of the three-story Moyamensing Prison that once held "Dr." Holmes after he was found guilty of murdering a co-conspirator (he also murdered three of his partner's children so they wouldn't raise suspicion to authorities). While in Philly, Holmes confessed to 27 murders, a figure researchers would later believe to be closer to 200. He met a cruel, perhaps deserving, end. Sentenced to hang, Holmes' neck refused to snap, resulting in 20 minutes of belabored twitching before he finally succumbed to the fate he inflicted upon so many others, all before his 35th birthday.

Address 1400 S 10th Street, Philadelphia, PA 19147, www.hmdb.org | Getting there
Bus 45 to Passyunk Avenue & 10th Street | Hours Unrestricted | Tip The inspiration for
Silence of the Lambs came from serial killer Gary Heidnik and his "house of horrors," located
in North Philly, and now apartments. If you're intent upon visiting this one, a drive by is
recommended rather than a walk (3520 N Marshall Street).

MOYAMENSING PRISON

Opened in 1835, Thomas U. Walter designed
it with elements of Egyptian Revival style
and following the revolutionary principle
of isolated confinement. With later additions, it could house nearly 5000 inmates
—African Americans and women in separate
wings. H. H. Holmes, considered America's
first serial killer, was executed here.
The last hanging in Pa. took place here in
1916, soon replaced by electrocution.
Closed in 1963, it was razed in 1968.

PENNSYLVANIA HISTORICAL AND MUSEUM COMMISSION 2011

30__East Market

A full community in a single block

Neighborhood boundaries change from time to time, often becoming more localized as they break into smaller communities. But exactly how small can a neighborhood be while still maintaining a unique identity worthy of its own name? In Philadelphia, the answer may be as small as a single block.

While we won't go as far as to call East Market a neighborhood, it's certainly a community – sometimes referred to as a micro-community. In this fully-redesigned district, you'll find offices, apartments, a snazzy hotel, and plenty of shops and restaurants, but it's the character of its public spaces that truly defines it. This is a social environment that beckons you to enjoy the tables and chairs along the Chestnut Walk promenade, especially when twinkling overhead lights illuminate the evenings. Swings are an option too. The shop windows are often dressed in murals and sculptures by Philadelphia artists, and the Canopy Hotel's restaurant, The Wayward, spills out into the scene, drawing you into the hotel that's well worth a peek.

This block was once the property of the fourth richest man in US history, Stephen Girard, and The Wayward's 19th-century Beaux-Arts style skyscraper-turned-hotel reflects the grandeur of its illustrious beginning. The reimagined interior offers a glimpse into the neighborhood's evolution. Design inspirations came from various periods and range from the glamorous department store and one-time world's largest clothing manufacturer, Snellenburg's, which was once its neighbor, to the Philadelphia hip-hop culture of the 1980s. Look for pop installations of luxury handbags and deflating basketballs, with quirky light fixtures hung over vibrant rugs and boldly-upholstered plush furniture throughout, in this mélange of styles that speaks to the address' long history in such a colorful city. Bonus: There's a Federal Donuts in the lobby.

Address 1100 Market Street, Philadelphia, PA 19107, www.eastmarket.com | Getting there Subway to 11th Street (Market–Frankford Line); Bus 17, 33, 44, 48 to Market & 11th Streets | Hours Unrestricted | Tip Federal Donuts is all over the city now, but you can still make a pilgrimage to the original in Pennsport for the best in doughnuts and Korean fried chicken (1219 2nd Street, www.federaldonuts.com).

31 Edgar Allan Poe's House
Three stories and one creepy basement

Don't come here expecting to find a preserved house filled with period pieces reimagining the life of one of the country's most famous writers. While Edgar Allan Poe's Philadelphia years were among his most prolific as an author and, as tour guides here may tell you, his happiest, he was the very definition of a starving artist with few possessions and a chronic inability to pay the rent on this humble house. Don't judge too hard, though.

Poe was one of America's first professional writers, depending exclusively on income from his words to pay his bills and blazing a trail for future authors and critics. Today, the house is even more stark than when he inhabited it with his wife, Virginia Eliza Clemm Poe, and mother-in-law, and there's been little attempt to glow up the home's bones in the past century, but consider this a gift as you tread the floors of the unglorified rooms. The house emanates a desolate and disturbed aura perfect for recalling your favorite scenes from Poe's more macabre pieces.

Still, this isn't just an empty house. Administered by the National Park Service with free ranger-led tours (self-guided exploration permitted, too), the three floors of original living space are now accompanied by neighboring buildings that include Poe exhibits, an educational short film, and a period-decorated reading room containing all of Poe's works, collectively comprising the complete Edgar Allan Poe National Historical Site.

Within the house itself, the can't-miss experience is a trip to the basement, especially for fans of *The Black Cat*. Poe lived in many houses throughout his seven years in Philly, but, while it's not entirely possible to nail down exactly which pieces were written from this house, *The Black Cat* does fall within this time frame, and the basement here is a ringer for the one described in the gruesome tale. Venture down the stairs and decide for yourself.

Address 532 N 7th Street, Philadelphia, PA 19123, +1 (215) 587-8780, www.nps.gov/edal | Getting there Bus 47 to 7th & Green Streets | Hours Fri–Sun 9am–noon & 1–5pm | Tip The Rare Book Department of the Free Library of Philadelphia contains one of the world's largest collections of Poe's writings and effects. It's by appointment only, but you can pop in to see the stuffed raven believed to have inspired his famous story (1901 Vine Street, libwww.freelibrary.org).

32 __ Eiffel Tower of Philly

It's a milk bottle, but close enough

The French may have something to say about Philadelphians calling this water tower atop the Harbisons Dairy complex the "Eiffel Tower of Philadelphia," but there's truly something to the moniker. The nickname was bestowed upon this structure by Oscar Beisert of the Keeping Society of Philadelphia for a successful bid to have the dairy complex protected with landmark status. The "Kensington milk bottle," as it's more widely known, is truly a defining symbol of the neighborhood, it's lit at night, and you can't say it doesn't share the same general shape as the Eiffel Tower in Paris.

Long visible to commuters from I-95, this iconic structure had been a rooftop stalwart for more than half a century before the interstate was even built. Erected in 1914 to advertise the dairy below, the water tower was exposed to the elements, and, for most of modern memory, it has been little more than a rusted reminder of the neighborhood's decline, well after Harbisons sold the building in the 1960s.

Today, though, the Kensington milk bottle represents something much brighter, and not just because the bottle itself has been brightened with fresh paint for the first time in decades. Restored and repainted to its historic appearance in 2018, the bright white and red bottle now stands as a symbol of the rebirth of the Kensington neighborhood, following the example of bordering Fishtown, which has positioned itself as the city's creative capital.

Within the formerly abandoned dairy buildings that remain, now protected with landmark status like the water tower above, Harbisons Dairy rents swoon-worthy, boutique apartments equipped with community amenities like a dog park, fitness center, and, of course, the furnished rooftop deck you'd demand from an address made famous by its water tower. Grab a coffee at the café and take a look at the revitalized tower that's saving a neighborhood.

Address 2041 Coral Street, Philadelphia, PA 19125, +1 (484) 904-1111, www.harbisonsdairy.com | **Getting there** Bus 3 to Front & Coral Streets, or 89 to Susquehanna Avenue & Coral Street | **Hours** Unrestricted | **Tip** Check out more historical industry at Philadelphia Brewing Co. nearby. The original brewery here was built in 1885, 20 years after Harbisons (2440 Frankford Avenue, www.philadelphiabrewing.com).

33 Emmy the Mannequin

A local celeb hawking inside jokes

There's a lot to unpack at South Fellini. While the shop's premise is simple enough – t-shirts, hoodies, pins, and patches – you won't be able to take a quick browse here and pop out a few minutes later. Like a candle shop that demands you sniff all its wares individually, the merch at South Fellini overflows with Philly-specific sayings, catchphrases, and inside jokes, and you'll easily lose an hour reading through them.

Someone new to town may be baffled by most of the content, but, if you truly belong here ("here" meaning both the city and the shop!), you'll be chuckling your way through every item.

The store's top draws include Wawa gear and anything emblazoned with the word "jawn," that most inexplicable yet universally applicable word in the Philly lexicon. It specializes in bringing vintage symbols of Philadelphia to contemporary residents, keeping that "I remember when …" spirit alive and well among Philly lifers. Picking up some gear here is also becoming something of a rite of passage for new residents looking for ways to show their local pride. If you have some clever ideas of your own, they do plenty of custom shirt and hoodie business here, too.

While *Mare of Easttown* may have put Wawa on the national map, and there's enough goose gear at South Fellini to satisfy even the most ardent devotee, the true Hollywood star of this South Philly shop is the unassuming Emmy. Modeling the best of local apparel, Emmy isn't just *a* mannequin, she's *the* mannequin. In 1987, Emmy starred in the film *Mannequin*, shot at the legendary Wanamaker Building, and her human counterpart was played by Kim Cattrall, most notably of *Sex and the City* fame. Shop co-owner Tony Trov previously worked for one of the film's crew, who later found her in a storage shed, rescued her from a life of isolation, and volunteered her for a modeling job at South Fellini.

Address 1507 E Passyunk Avenue, Philadelphia, PA 19147, +1 (267) 751-3667, www.tshirtsphiladelphia.com | Getting there Bus 45 to Passyunk Avenue & Dickinson Street | Hours Mon–Fri 11am–7pm, Sat 10am–7pm, Sun 10am–6pm | Tip Macy's at The Wanamaker Building is still home to the world's largest fully-functioning pipe organ, and it's played twice daily, Monday–Saturday (1300 Market Street, www.wanamakerorgan.com).

34 _ Eternal Performance
Some seats come with an extra show

The Academy of Music is no secret spot in Philadelphia. Opened in 1857, it's the oldest opera house still holding performances in the US today, and it lays claim to the even more impressive title of oldest playhouse still performing in the entire English-speaking world. Modeled after La Scala in Milan, this dramatic treasure is respected worldwide and has long been loved by Philly residents. But some may adore The Academy a little too ardently.

It's an old city (by American standards) and an old building, so rumors of hauntings are all but guaranteed. Reports from this venue aren't the run-of-the-mill tales of phantom voices and mysterious footsteps. While plenty of older theaters report long-dead actors who continue to tread the boards or cause mischief for prop masters, the spirits who remain behind at The Academy are generally found among the audience. That's good news if you're looking for a supernatural encounter and can't score a backstage tour! Even better news? The tickets you'll need to purchase are among the least expensive in the house (not that you'll regret taking in a world-class performance in his venerable hall, regardless).

Head to the amphitheater, the uppermost deck, if the performance you seek involves more than the stage alone. Here, patrons have reported unoccupied seats around them suddenly becoming indented or wrinkled in, well, the shape of someone's butt, as though invisible music lovers had just arrived to take in the show. A bit less subtle, others have reported being pinched or having their hair pulled on the amphitheater level, and witnesses even claim to have seen the inexplicable hair-pulling happen to these unsuspecting audience members.

Unfortunately, there's no solid record of who these victims or witnesses were, so this story is likely to be mere legend, but it certainly adds a new level of intrigue to a night at the theater here.

Address 240 S Broad Street, Philadelphia, PA 19102, +1 (215) 893-1999, www.academyofmusic.org | Getting there Subway to Walnut–Locust (Broad Street Line); Bus 4, 27, 32 to Broad & Locust Streets | Hours See website for performance schedule | Tip Swap the historical for the more contemporary across the street with a visit to The Wilma Theater, named for a fictional sister of Shakespeare imagined by Virginia Woolf (265 S Broad Street, www.wilmatheater.org).

35 Fairmount Groot

An enduring fixture in an evolving garden

Take a stroll along Fairmount Avenue between 16th and 17th Streets, and you'll come upon the whimsical garden of Keith Grabowsky, Philly resident of more than a decade, whose Fairmount display has become a neighborhood magnet. What started with the slow revival of a raised sidewalk garden in 2018 truly blossomed when Grabowsky added a miniature of Groot of Marvel Comics fame, in 2019. A fountain, lights, and plenty of colorful friends, from latte-sipping frogs to Bernie Sanders in his inauguration day chair, have joined Groot in the years since his debut. You can expect to find upwards of 50 characters hidden among the foliage and formations of the family garden today.

While his wife and two children are involved, the family says this garden is truly Grabowsky's labor of love, and it's certainly brought the neighborhood a little closer together as people check in while passing along the busy sidewalk on errands, or even come by specifically to see what's new in the garden. Like the little weatherproof library boxes that have popped up in neighborhoods across the nation and the world, offering strangers the chance to leave behind old favorites or pick up new ones, people occasionally leave new characters in the garden as they pass by, which means not even the family necessarily knows *everything* that calls its beloved garden home at any given time.

Grabowsky also rotates some characters seasonally, and other times just for fun. As Groot was the first personality to enter the fantasy-scape, his place in the garden has been decreed as permanent, having become something of an honorary garden ambassador to the community, so you'll always find him here. He even has his own Instagram account (@fairmountgroot). Oh, and what's Grabowsky's secret to maintaining not just a fun, but genuinely healthy garden without much of a green thumb to speak of? Succulents.

Address 1615 Fairmount Avenue, Philadelphia, PA 19130, www.instagram.com/
fairmountgroot | Getting there Subway to Fairmount (Broad Street Line); Bus 2 to
16th Street & Fairmount Avenue | Hours Unrestricted from the outside only | Tip If you're
looking to add to the garden, you might find something appropriately quirky at Ali's Wagon,
less than a 10-minute walk from here (2017 Fairmount Avenue, www.aliswagon.com).

36__Fairmount Water Works

A hands-on learning center in a historic location

The Schuylkill River's most renowned landmark is undoubtedly its shimmering Boathouse Row, but you'll have to look next door to find one of Philadelphia's first major tourist attractions. Today, the Fairmount Water Works Interpretive Center draws a fraction of the attention of Boathouse Row and the Philadelphia Museum of Art, its other neighbor, but it's working on a worthy comeback.

In 1815, the Water Works opened as the world's first modern municipal water-pumping station dressed in exteriors of Classical Revival architecture. Combined with meticulously-sculpted grounds that soon became the largest landscaped urban park in North America, the facility ultimately transformed the Schuylkill riverbank into something of a nostalgic pleasure garden, disguising the industrial labor within. The gorgeous grounds propelled the water facility to top tourism status, attracting international celebrities like Charles Dickens before it was decommissioned in 1909.

With most of the machinery removed, the exteriors have been revived several times for varied uses during their two centuries. In 1911, the grounds reopened as the Philadelphia Aquarium and remained open for just over 50 years before the Kelly Natatorium, a swimming pool originally used for the private Olympic training of the Kelly family (as in Grace Kelly, Princess of Monaco) dominated the next decade. The pool would eventually open to the public and hold the distinction of being Philadelphia's first integrated pool. Hurricane Agnes fatally damaged it in 1972.

Today, you'll find hands-on programming generating potentially surprising interest in the Philadelphia urban watershed at the modern education center now based at Water Works. Stop in for tours, lectures, or exhibits, and participate in the field-trip-style programs conducted in and around the area's waterways for truly immersive education.

Address 640 Waterworks Drive, Philadelphia, PA 19130, +1 (215) 685-0723, www.fairmountwaterworks.org | **Getting there** Bus 38 to Art Museum Drive & Spring Garden Street | **Hours** Wed–Fri 11am–5pm, Sat 10am–5pm | **Tip** Philly no longer has its own aquarium, so take the RiverLink Ferry to the Adventure Aquarium in Camden, New Jersey, a worthy replacement (1 Riverside Drive, Camden, www.adventureaquarium.com).

37 FDR Skate Park

Where community and government agree

FDR Park is South Philadelphia's largest park, and one of its coolest features lies along its southeast corner. Here, underneath the I-95 overpass, the city erected some barebones skateboarding features in 1996 in an attempt to shift attention away from Love Park's reputation as a premier skating destination (skating is now banned there, but that hasn't stopped international enthusiasts from making regular pilgrimages at the risk of fines and board confiscation). Unfortunately, the obstacles provided were poorly constructed and not very exciting, so the park was largely ignored by local street skaters – until they took matters into their own hands.

Over time, skaters themselves began toying with construction in this largely ignored section of the park and were surprised to find they were met with little resistance from the city. Ultimately, FDR Skate Park would come to be *the* park for Philadelphia skaters, and it was almost entirely conceived and funded by volunteer efforts.

It's still maintained by volunteers today, having expanded beyond the original overpass core to include multiple new zones that now comprise the world's largest DIY skate park. In 2019, Philadelphia announced a $200 million renovation of FDR Park, and some feared the city's *laissez-faire* attitude toward the skate park would come to an end. But local government appeared to have recognized the value this venue brought to the community and vowed to leave it untouched and largely ungoverned.

You don't need to be a skater yourself to enjoy this concrete oasis bordering the Navy Yard. Regardless of your age or skating ability, come for the sheer visual spectacle of this maze of obstacles covered in an explosion of ever-changing graffiti that showers its gray bones in color. The energy here is of self-made celebration and camaraderie – something Philly does best when its communities work together.

Address 1500 Pattison Avenue, Philadelphia, PA 19145, +1 (215) 462-8997, www.fdrparkphilly.org/skatepark | **Getting there** Subway to NRG (Broad Street Line); Bus 17 to Pattison Avenue & 20th Street | **Hours** Apr–Oct, daily 6am–9pm, Nov–Mar, daily 6am–6pm | **Tip** Paine's Park offers an additional 30,000 square feet of skating obstacles along the Schuylkill River (Martin Luther King Jr. Drive & Benjamin Franklin Parkway, www.visitphilly.com).

38 First Antislavery Protest
An early petition against hypocrisy and injustice

Among the best-known abolitionists in US history, the most enduring names come to us from the 19th century – but not all waited quite so long to speak up. In fact, plenty petitioned against the enslavement of other humans before the colonies even became states, and the first known example came from Philadelphia, just six years after the city was founded.

The Quakers are a famously peaceful group and were among the very earliest settlers of Philadelphia, but not all of them agreed on the issue of slavery. Those Quakers from Britain, where slavery was commonplace, brought enslaved people with them to Pennsylvania. But the German Quakers were unaccustomed to slavery and took immediate objection to the barbaric practice. Offended and outraged by their own brethren, the Quakers of what was already called Germantown penned a petition to ban slavery and presented it at their monthly meeting in 1688. In an all-too-typical game of passing the buck, the issue was elevated to the more important quarterly meeting, and again to the annual meeting, with even this governing body refusing to decide.

Undaunted, the Germantown Quakers refused to allow slavery within their community and continued in business and religious life in stark contrast to their British counterparts until Quakers finally banned the practice entirely among their members in 1776. It had been nearly 90 years since the Germantown Quakers' original protest, but the group still managed to abolish this inhumane injustice almost 90 years before the United States would do the same nationwide.

Today, nearly 350 years after the New World's first documented protest against slavery, the table on which this culture-defying document was signed remains, standing quietly on display within the Germantown Mennonite Meetinghouse, a sturdy reminder of the enduring power of conscience and the determination of Philadelphia.

Address 6133 Germantown Avenue, Philadelphia, PA 19144, +1 (215) 843-0943, www.meetinghouse.info, gmht@meetinghouse.info | Getting there Bus 23 to Germantown Avenue & Tulpehocken Street | Hours See website for tours and events | Tip Down the street, Germantown Town Hall is an architecturally-striking local landmark that has been abandoned for decades, despite intermittent interest from developers (Germantown Avenue & W Haines Street).

39 First Person Arts

Where Philadelphians take center stage

If a destination is defined by its people, then a visit to First Person Arts (FPA) is the quickest and most intimate way to uncover the true nature of Philadelphia. Dedicated to personal narrative, FPA is best known for its storytelling events but doesn't limit its scope to any specific artforms, instead embracing "artists who tell their true, personal stories in any medium," according to FPA marketing manager, Samantha Heth. You can meet her and other staff at most FPA events, as they regularly mingle with the audience, eager to connect with attendees.

You'll have a hard time locating the First Person Arts venue because, well, there isn't one. Instead of hosting events at a permanent location, FPA seeks venues ideally matched to the size, type, and audience of each show, consciously seeking to embrace as many Philadelphia neighborhoods as possible to connect the community. You can expect to find events popping up at bars, libraries, stages, and just about anywhere a group can come together to experience the intimacy of personal narrative in any format.

If stability is your style, you'll be most interested in FPA's regular schedule of monthly StorySlams, where audience members throw their names in a bucket for a chance to share their stories during these themed events. Heth suggests building your confidence and preparedness by writing and practicing your story a bit before attending, but she acknowledges that it's not a firm rule. "Sometimes inspiration will strike you when you walk in the door or at intermission, after you've seen some storytellers perform. If you have a feeling somewhere inside of you, we encourage you to listen to that and put your name in the bucket because that's the first step to getting on stage!" You don't need to have a desire to share in order to attend, though. All that's required of audiences is an open mind and a supportive attitude.

40 Fitler Square Farmers Market

A delicious secret in a picturesque square

Fitler Square is a delightful half-acre park surrounded by the equally lovely neighborhood of the same name. The pathways between its dainty lawns and trees are home to two local treasures. If you're familiar with the park, you already know one of them: the sculpture collection. Here you'll find several sculpted animals, including a grizzly bear and family of three turtles by Eric Berg, whose bronze warthog lives at the Philadelphia Zoo, and a ram by Gerd Hesness. Look for a charming, Victorian-era fountain at the park's center. But the neighborhood's best kept secret isn't visual. It's edible.

Since 2003, Fitler Square has hosted a year-round farmers market held every Saturday, weather permitting. The market typically presents just two vendors at a time, sourcing eligible farmers from Pennsylvania, New Jersey, Delaware, Maryland, and New York. The market's longest-running partner is Brogue Hydroponics, which offers its hydroponically-grown produce and also perennials and summer flower bouquets seasonally. The farm has been with the market since the beginning, and Meghan Filoromo of The Food Trust's Farmers Market Program says their fresh ginger and turmeric roots are highlights of the market in fall.

Not all vendors are farmers here, though. Like most markets today, you'll encounter prepared foods from local businesses at Fitler Square, too. On any given week, you may find Argentinian empanadas, Brazilian pastries, or even kombucha. Native plant vendors aren't uncommon, either. The Food Trust, which operates the market, is dedicated to equal access to nutrition, so market vendors accept benefits from most local food subsidy programs. If you've watched M. Night Shyamalan's *Servant*, you may have spotted the park several times through the seasons.

Address S 23rd Street & Pine Street, Philadelphia, PA 19103, +1 (215) 575-0444, www.thefoodtrust.org, contact@thefoodtrust.org | Getting there Bus 7, 12 to 23rd & Pine Streets | Hours Sat 9am–2pm | Tip You can visit Eric Berg's winter studio in Philly to check out more of his work, by appointment only (3823 Baring Street, www.bergbronze.com).

41 __ Fletcher Street Urban Riding Club

Philly's urban Black cowboys

Despite generations of Hollywood Westerns, it's estimated that up to 25 percent of all cowboys were Black. And cowboys didn't all live and work in the Wild West. Philadelphia's population of Black cowboys was primarily formed in the early 1900s, and they're still here, though their work has changed.

Many of Philly's original Black cowboys arrived from the struggling South, seeking jobs in the busy, industrial North, and they brought their animals with them. Plenty continued on to settle the West, but many remained in the city, driving carriages or making deliveries by horse. It wasn't long before engine horsepower replaced equine horsepower, though, and Northern owners began regularly auctioning off their unneeded and ill-fated horses. Philly's Black cowboys, however, mounted what would become a decades-long tradition of rescuing doomed horses and stabling them safely within the city – a hallmark of today's remaining urban cowboy community, too.

While the number of Black riding clubs in Philadelphia has dwindled, its most storied remains. Fletcher Street Urban Riding Club (FSURC), with history dating back more than a century, is now a non-profit primarily serving the city's Black youth. Founder Ellis Ferrell says spending time at the stables gives neighborhood kids an alternative to the streets, and learning to tend and ride horses develops discipline, dedication, and purpose. It's also a form of therapy.

If you've seen Black cowboys riding horses through the streets of Strawberry Mansion and beyond, or in Fairmount Park, they were probably members of FSURC. You may also recognize some of their faces from the 2020 film *Concrete Cowboy*. Stable tours are available by appointment via email, and they're always accepting new members, too.

Address 2607–11 W Fletcher Street, Philadelphia, PA 19132, +1 (800) 484-1930, www.fsurc.com, info@fsurc.com | Getting there Bus 7, 39 to Dauphin & 26th Streets | Hours Mon–Fri by appointment only, Sat & Sun 8am–2pm | Tip To take a recreational ride, visit Chamounix Equestrian Center in West Fairmount Park, where all ages and experience levels are welcome (98 Chamounix Drive, www.worktoride.net).

42 Four Seasons Total Landscaping

A political disaster and a business boon

November 2020 was a tense time in the US, as a fiercely-contested presidential election captivated the nation. Tenuous relationships that had somehow survived the previous four years were stretched to the breaking point, but one day in particular sealed the fate of the then-president's re-election efforts. On November 7, his campaign held a press conference outside a landscaper's garage.

Pennsylvania's electoral college votes were critical, and Philadelphia's remaining ballots were being counted at the Four Seasons Hotel Philadelphia. In protest of alleged voter fraud in Pennsylvania (despite no evidence then or since), the Trump legal team planned a press conference onsite. Though organizers have yet to admit this was a mistake, the event was inadvertently booked at Four Seasons Total Landscaping.

And so the press conference was indeed held in the small business' parking lot, a poster-peppered garage door serving as the backdrop for the podium. The enormity of this oversight was symbolic enough of the chaos and desperation within the failed campaign, but the AP delivered a final blow when it projected Biden as the winner of Pennsylvania's electoral votes and therefore the national election *during* the press conference. Media began departing immediately.

Four Seasons Total Landscaping, suddenly the country's most famous small business, is a woman-owned, minority-owned commercial landscaper that declared no political agenda when hosting the conference and capitalized on the event with savvy and humor. Aside from the invaluable free publicity that stemmed from international news coverage, the team quickly launched a line of merchandise that raked in more than $1.3 million in its first few weeks alone and started a summer concert series the following year.

Address 7339 State Road, Philadelphia, PA 19136, +1 (215) 624-5408, www.fstl1992.com |
Getting there Bus 70 to State Road & Bleigh Avenue | Hours Mon–Fri 8am–4pm;
unrestricted from the outside | Tip To see the real Four Seasons Hotel Philadelphia, where
Philly's votes decided the national election, head to the Comcast Center (1 N 19th Street,
www.fourseasons.com/philadelphia).

43__George Washington's Apron

For ceremony, not for kitchen messes

No, the first president of the United States was not a prolific baker, toiling away in a kitchen apron, though he did run one of the country's largest whiskey distilleries from his Mount Vernon estate. Still, George Washington did wear an apron on occasion, albeit a ceremonial one, particularly when attending meetings at Masonic lodges. While the Illuminati may be the secret society *du jour*, capturing pop culture's collective imagination frequently, the symbolism, ceremonies, and unquestionable prestige of Freemasonry's more famous members have kept it in the spotlight for centuries. And the Masons are verifiably real. So real, in fact, that you can visit The Masonic Library and Museum of Pennsylvania yourself, and you don't even need to be a member. Honestly – just walk in.

The Freemasons have historically been surrounded by mystery and secrecy, but you wouldn't know it from the openness of its towering temple complex in Philadelphia. Not only is the temple itself open to the public for tours and easily rented for special events, but the contents of its comprehensive library are equally accessible. Access to the vast history of Freemasonry found within this trove is surprisingly easy, but we can certainly assume there are plenty of secrets *not* cached here.

While there are some true treasures among the library's holdings, including a book printed in 1489 (that's an "incunabulum," for you bibliophiles), it's the museum you'll want to visit in order to gawk at notable objects. Among the 30,000 pieces in this collection, you'll find Washington's Masonic apron, presented to him by the Marquis de Lafayette, as well as the sash Benjamin Franklin wore when he inducted Voltaire into the esteemed society. Both the Library and Museum are collectively known as the John Wanamaker Resource Center, named for the local merchant who dedicated it.

Address 1 N Broad Street, Philadelphia, PA 19107, +1 (215) 988-1900, www.pamasonictemple.org, lmuseum@pagrandlodge.org | Getting there Subway to 13th Street (Market–Frankford Line); Bus 4, 16 to Broad & Arch Streets | Hours See website for tour schedule | Tip Directly across the street, City Hall is teeming with Masonic influence. The cornerstone was laid by a Mason, while another Mason was mayor of Philadelphia, and the architect and design assistant were Masons, too (1400 John F. Kennedy Boulevard, www.phila.gov).

44_ Germantown White House

America's oldest surviving presidential residence

The phrase "George Washington slept here" may be little more than a sarcastic quip across America today, but if you've spent any considerable amount of time in Southeastern Pennsylvania and its immediate surroundings, you've likely seen a house or two where this was true. One house in Philadelphia has an even greater claim to early American history: the Deshler-Morris House in the city's Germantown section was home to the country's most revered president *while* he was governing. Twice.

Though President Washington oversaw the construction of the White House in Washington, DC, it wasn't completed until 1800, when John and Abigail Adams took up residence in the executive mansion. Without today's gleaming behemoth available, Washington spent his two terms serving from the nations' first two capitals, New York City and Philadelphia, respectively, with annual visits to his Mount Vernon home in Virginia. On his return from Mount Vernon in 1793, he found Philadelphia under quarantine due to the yellow fever epidemic and settled on the Deshler-Morris House for temporary residence. The following year, he returned to the quiet house to escape the summer heat of downtown Philadelphia and governed from Germantown once again.

President Washington isn't the only celebrated figure to have spent time in this house. Because he governed the new nation from this spot, other notable figures in post-Revolution history made the short journey for cabinet meetings, Alexander Hamilton and Thomas Jefferson among them.

The house's final owner, Elliston P. Morris, donated the property to the National Park Service in 1948, and it joined the National Register of Historic Places in 1972. Today, the interiors have been restored to 18th-century style, and the site is open seasonally.

Address 5442 Germantown Avenue, Philadelphia, PA 19144, +1 (215) 596-1748, www.nps.gov/inde/planyourvisit/germantownwhitehouse.htm | **Getting there** Light Rail to Germantown (Chestnut Hill East Line); Bus 23 to Germantown Avenue & School House Lane | **Hours** See website for tour hours | **Tip** The even lesser-known Bringhurst House is next door. Bringhurst built a carriage for the president during his time here, and there are some exhibits on the Washington household within the surviving house (5448 Germantown Avenue).

45 Giant Otters
Philadelphia's cutest "first"

If you're from Philly, you already know that the Philadelphia Zoo was the country's first true zoo. It's far from a hidden gem in the local community. But there's a national community that owes its very existence to our beloved zoological garden, and that's the giant otter community.

River otters were once plentiful in Pennsylvania but, by the mid 1900s, not only were they hard to find in the wild, but zoos across the United States hardly had them. *Giant* otters are native only to select South American river systems and are an endangered species, a fact that snagged the attention of the Philly Zoo when it shifted its primary focus to conservation in the 1990s. The zoo invited their first otters in 70 years to live on the property, one of only two zoos in the nation to display river otters at all at the time.

In 2002, the zoo in Brasilia, Brazil sent a female to Philly. Two years later, the aptly-named Primero became the first giant otter born in North America. In time, Primero was followed by a whopping nineteen siblings (three of whom still live here today!), mating and raising otter pups of their own. Many went on to zoos around the country, in cities like Houston, Miami, and Los Angeles. While Philly is responsible for spearheading this national community of giant otters still spreading across the United States, all giant otters born at our zoo are still technically the property of the Brazilian government and are considered "on loan," like the giant pandas at the National Zoo in Washington, DC.

Today, giant otters have arguably the most fun habitat at the Philadelphia Zoo, with connecting pools and a splashtastic water slide – a fitting palace for the first family of North American giant otters. They're most active early in the morning and late in the day (plus feeding time, of course!), so you're likely to catch some action whenever you visit.

Address 3400 W Girard Avenue, Philadelphia, PA 19104, +1 (215) 243-1100, www.philadelphiazoo.org | Getting there Light Rail to W Girard Avenue & N 34th Street (15 Line) | Hours Daily 9:30am–5pm | Tip If you want to try your luck at otter spotting in the wild (and you *will* need some luck), the best place to do this is by the Fairmount fish ladder at Fairmount Dam at twilight (Fairmount Dam & West River Drive, www.schuylkillbanks.org).

46_ Giant Wood Slide

Big fun for the little ones

The Smith Memorial Playground is a modern play utopia with historic roots. Now with more than 50 pieces of accessible play equipment across 6.5 acres of outdoor space, it's also home to a 16,000-square-foot, three-level playhouse with additional indoor space that was renovated and reopened in early 2022. As one of the country's first dedicated play spaces, Smith is primarily devoted to maintaining a healthy environment for unstructured play in urban nature. It also advocates for community-building and education by offering regular programming, both on-site and off, conceived by Smith's team of child development and play experts.

The site was dedicated in 1899, but it's a 1905 introduction that still brings the biggest smiles today. At 12.5 feet wide and 40 feet long, the Ann Newman Giant Wooden Slide is exactly what it sounds like. The regularly waxed wooden boards of this epic slide, which looks more like a sloped bowling lane, have been known to offer some serious speed, as far as slides go. It's suggested that you use the provided burlap sacks to help protect the wood and to get more wind in your hair. Most people tend to comply, but there's one suggestion that frequently gets ignored, and the organization is okay with that. While the slide is recommended for those 12 and under, director of development Danielle Smith says they don't turn away older kids or parents who want to get in on the fun. She says you'll find teens and adults sliding any time you visit, so feel free to try it out no matter your age (though it's probably best if you're visiting *with* a child!).

Like all of Smith Memorial Playground's offerings, the Giant Wooden Slide is free, and the non-profit relies completely on donations, fundraising, and grants. If you can't get enough of the slide, consider helping them fundraise by joining the annual Slide-A-Thon in spring.

Address 3500 Reservoir Drive, Philadelphia, PA 19121, +1 (215) 765-4325, www.smithplayground.org, info@smithplayground.org | Getting there Bus 3 to Reservoir & Smith Day Nursery Drives | Hours Tue–Fri 10am–6pm, Sat & Sun 10am–7pm | Tip The playground's namesake, Richard Smith, made his fortune in typesetting while Philadelphia served as the printing and publishing capital of America. Franklin Court offers free demonstrations of 18th-century printing daily (322 Market Street, www.nps.gov).

47 _ Graffiti Pier

Philly's most photographed illegal art

What's often claimed to be Philadelphia's most Instagrammed location is not exactly a welcoming environment for visitors. In fact, it's illegal to trespass on this private property, making it all the more appealing to the graffiti artists who tag, stencil, sketch, and paint it, and to the curious gawkers who skulk about for a glimpse.

Graffiti Pier is a former Conrail coal-loading dock on the Delaware River that was closed in the early 1990s and has sat abandoned – but certainly not undisturbed – ever since. Largely unmonitored through most of its decaying years, the towering concrete structure served as a frequent canvas for graffiti artists of varying skill levels through the decades, with the arched arcade on the lower level positively covered in tantalizing color. In more recent years, as the structure began deteriorating more rapidly and a spate of violent crime in the area raised additional concerns, trespassing has been taken considerably more seriously and the site is regularly patrolled. But all is not lost.

The Delaware River Waterfront Corporation is currently developing plans to stabilize the pier and open a park, legalizing graffiti on surfaces within and providing safe access to the public. While an opening date isn't yet available, the planning committee confirms it will take several years of labor after a design is finalized, so an opening is not anticipated until at least 2024. The original structure isn't expected to be changed much beyond stabilization and safety concerns, but the area itself will be more pleasingly planted (including the currently hard-to-reach second level), restrooms and lighting will be added, an event space is likely, and more surfaces will be made available for graffiti.

Until then, you can legally and safely preview some of the current illicit artwork from the river, from the road, and from neighboring piers.

Address E Cumberland Street, Philadelphia, PA 19125, +1 (215) 922-2386, www.delawareriverwaterfront.com | Getting there Bus 39 to Cumberland & Richmond Streets | Hours Unrestricted from the outside only | Tip For curated street art, try Sharktown Walls in Kensington (1701 N Hancock Street).

48 _ *The Gross Clinic*
So gross it couldn't be displayed

Its evocative name is a matter of mere coincidence, but *The Gross Clinic*, a painting by Thomas Eakins, was indeed considered too gross to display when first presented to the selection committee of the 1876 Centennial Exhibition in Philadelphia. Intending to demonstrate Philadelphia's leadership in science and education, Eakin's subject is Dr. Samuel Gross performing a gruesome operation for the benefit of a class in the surgical amphitheater of Jefferson Medical College. Art appreciators of the day were not accustomed to this style of in-your-face veritas that would later be dubbed "scientific realism".

While you may not find anything particularly disturbing about this painting as a modern viewer, an incision and some bloody fingertips were apparently too shocking for the art-loving public and was relegated to an army field hospital exhibit instead. There, critics discovered the 8-foot by 6.5-foot painting that would later go on to be dubbed by the *New York Times* as "hands down, the finest 19th century American painting." The painting was also noted to be of higher quality than any work the selection committee did approve. It was purchased for $200 and donated to Jefferson Medical College, where Eakins himself studied and could view his masterpiece.

In 2006, in need of funding, Jefferson arranged to sell the painting for $68 million, a record for a pre-WWII artwork from the United States. Philadelphians rallied to stop the sale by producing the staggering amount themselves and managed to raise about half from donations in just a few weeks. The rest came when the Philadelphia Museum of Art and the Pennsylvania Academy of Fine Arts sold other works in their collections to raise the difference. Today, these two pillars of the Philly art scene share the painting. It hangs most regularly at PMA and travels to the Academy of Fine Arts for select exhibitions.

Address 2600 Benjamin Franklin Parkway, Philadelphia, PA 19130, +1 (215) 763-8100, www.philamuseum.org, visitorservices@philamuseum.org | Getting there Bus 43 to Spring Garden Street & Kelly Drive | Hours Thu & Sat–Mon 10am–5pm, Fri 10am–8:45pm | Tip The Thomas Eakins House (and studio) was added to the National Register of Historic Places in 1966 and is designated with a historical marker today (1729 Mount Vernon Street).

49 __ Halloween
Find the store, find a treasure

No matter how good your eyes are, you're not going to find the sign for Halloween, a shop that has very little to do with Halloween at all but is nearly as mysterious. To begin with, there is no sign for this shop. There's also no website, and owner Henri David says he's never advertised for the store since opening in 1990. It's all word of mouth, and that's the way he prefers it. So how do you find it, and what even is it? It's a densely-packed wonder of a jewelry shop. And, if you're lucky, there might be a dragon sculpture out front when you pass by the otherwise nondescript door. (Hint: it's on the corner of Juniper Street.)

Henri David's fascination with jewelry began when he was a costume boy at age 12. Today, he designs upwards of 40% of the pieces found at Halloween. And speaking of costumes, while the store sells neither Halloween costumes nor decorations, David is the founder of Philadelphia's legendary Halloween Ball, which he's been hosting since 1968 and for which he's perhaps most famous. Still, the shop is as much a spectacle and intrigue as any Halloween party, with displays covering every imaginable surface, built into pillars, walls, and more, and often arranged by themes that catch David's attention, like modes of transportation, hearts, the garden.

Minimalism is not the name of the game while treasure hunting at Halloween, so give yourself ample time to take a good, long look around the shop – and don't be concerned about budget. David may be a custom jewelry designer, and feel free to consult if you have a piece in mind. But he believes that beautiful jewelry doesn't have to put you in debt, which is perhaps why his clients range from celebrities all the way to young creatives just stepping out in the world. Here, it's about finding a piece that's meant for you, and there are no other rules. Oh, except that it must be handmade. You won't find anything else at Halloween.

Address 1329 Pine Street, Philadelphia, PA 19107, +1 (215) 732-7711 | Getting the
Bus 40 to Pine & 13th Streets | Hours Tue – Fri noon – 6pm, Sat 11am – 4pm | Tip
spectacular costume for Halloween or any other occasion, Pierre's Mascots & Costu
has more than one million pieces for rent and also designs originals (211 N 3rd Stre
www.costumers.com).

50 __ Hamilton Garden

A rooftop within a rooftop

If you've ever been to the Kimmel Center for the Performing Arts, you've no doubt already been amazed by its construction alone. With two independent venues, a theater and music hall, both enveloped by an enormous glass vault stretching 150 feet up into the city skyline, the extravagance of this deceptively simple design is enough reason to stop in for a peek. But there is also a best-kept secret to be found here, and you don't need to be attending a performance to catch it (though you can certainly do that, too).

One of Philadelphia's most magical rooftop views is found within the Kimmel Center – yes, that's "within" and not "atop." Take an elevator to the top of the Perelman Theater at the Center's entrance, and you'll find yourself standing on a full-fledged rooftop, while a second roof shelters you from, somehow, still higher overhead. Because the exterior arch encapsulating the center is glass, this rooftop atrium above the Perelman stays sheltered without detracting from one of the most glittering views in Center City.

The lofty rooftop garden is named for Dorrance H. Hamilton (1928 – 2017), who was a generous patron of the Kimmel Center. She was one of the wealthiest people in the United States, inheriting her fortune through her grandfather, who bought the Campbell Soup Company in 1914. Previously, this space was home to a potted-tree atrium that sat largely unvisited by a citizenry that didn't really know it was there. The trees are gone, and it's since been further walled in with glass to become a glitzy, 6,200-square-foot event space in an effort to maximize revenue for the Kimmel Cultural Campus. So you can't typically zip up here unaccompanied anymore.

However, you can still view and experience the space by taking a free tour of the Kimmel Center. Make your plans well in advance of your visit, though, because the center's spaces are available to rent for private events to help fund its programming.

Address 300 S Broad Street, Philadelphia, PA 19102, +1 (215) 790-5800, www.kimmelculturalcampus.org, patronservices@ticketphiladelphia.org | Getting there Bus 4, 27, 32 to Broad & Pine Streets | Hours Tours Daily 1pm, see website for monthly architecture tours | Tip For some actual Hamilton influence, check out the First Bank of the United States. It was his idea as first Secretary of the Treasury, and not one that was easily swallowed at the time (120 S 3rd Street, www.nps.gov).

51 Insectarium

The only cockroach kitchen you'd pay to see

You can pretend this one is for the kids, but it's all-ages intrigue at the Philadelphia Insectarium and Butterfly Pavilion. Whether you'll find more delight or disgust here is anyone's guess, but Philly's Insectarium is home to one of the most diverse living arthropod collections in the country, where you'll find everything from the gorgeous to the grotesque in this creepy crawly science center.

The Insectarium believes that arthropods are the most important group of animals in the world and aims to educate visitors on their critical ecological importance through two floors of exhibits and daily special events, including handling reptiles and tarantulas, cheering on roach races, and testing a scorpion's glow-in-the-dark ability. Among the many exhibits you'll encounter here, the grossest is undoubtedly the cockroach kitchen, which is exactly as it sounds: a filthy kitchen crawling with live cockroaches of all shapes and sizes (it's behind glass).

The most beautiful and certainly the main event for most guests is the 7,000-square-foot butterfly pavilion enclosing a tropical ecosphere of colorful plants, waterfalls, and a perpetual 80-degree climate. If you want to improve your odds of butterflies alighting on your shoulders, wear bright colors, and check the event calendar regularly for special experiences like butterfly yoga.

Elsewhere, you'll find an ant graveyard and a see-through honey beehive highlighting the work of the museum's most important-to-humans residents who, by the way, are actual working bees that leave the museum to pollinate and gather in the green spaces nearby throughout the day.

If you want to take some of the excitement home with you, grab a package of baked cheddar mealworms from the giftshop on your way out. They're organically grown, and, while they don't taste like much, you'll earn some solid bragging rights as you crunch away.

Address 8046 Frankford Avenue, Philadelphia, PA 19136, +1 (215) 335-9500, www.phillybutterflypavilion.com, info@phillybutterflypavilion.com | Getting there Bus 66 to Frankford Avenue & Welsh Road | Hours Daily 10am–5pm | Tip Want to get hands-on with honeybees? The Philadelphia Beekeepers Guild offers classes that include lessons at the Awbury Arboretum (6336 Ardleigh Street, www.phillybeekeepers.org).

52 Irish Memorial

A waterfront homage to those who came and went

Conversations about Philadelphia's immigrant history often center around the Germans and British of the colonial period and the Italians of the early 20th century. But the city is also home to the country's third largest Irish population, many of whose families arrived as a result of the Great Famine of the 1840s.

Upwards of one million Irish people fled to the United States to escape the starvation and disease that spread across their homeland during this period, and nearly 100,000 of them chose Philadelphia as their new home. Today, nearly 15% of the city claims Irish heritage, but it wasn't until 2003, the sesquicentennial of the famine, that Philadelphia publicly honored one of its largest ethnic groups with the monumental Irish Memorial at Penn's Landing, where many of the earliest Irish Americans first arrived.

Conceived and sculpted by Glenna Goodacre, best known for the Vietnam Women's Memorial in Washington, DC, the memorial consists of a staggering 35 life-sized bronze figures across a 30-foot by 12-foot by 12-foot amalgamation of scenes depicting the scope of emigration from starvation in Ireland to arrival in America, including scores of deaths along the journey. Though the memorial and the surrounding park also honor the contributions of Irish Americans, this is not a celebratory memorial. It tells the tragic tale not just of famine and death, but of the British abuse that resulted in the loss of 25% of Ireland's population, and of the brutal hostility America's desperate new immigrants faced.

Part of the memorial's emotional genius is that you can't simply stand and observe this piece. You need to take an active role in the experience, moving about its full circumference and confronting new vignettes as you go. Find the eight informational plinths stationed among the surrounding walkways, each describing an element of the Great Hunger and its aftermath.

Address 100 Chestnut Street, Philadelphia, PA 1910, www.irishmemorial.org | Getting there Bus 21, 42 to Chestnut & Front Streets | Hours Unrestricted | Tip Goodacre's relief of Sacagawea appears on the golden dollar coin issued in the early 2000s and struck at the Philadelphia Mint, one of only two United States Mint locations to offer tours (151 N Independence Mall E, www.usmint.gov/about).

53 Jazz Attack

Lindy Hop or Philly Bop, it's your call

Lindy Hop is a swing dance style that originated in the Black community of Harlem in the 1920s. It wasn't long before it traveled to Philadelphia, and the Philly Bop was born. If you want to learn the difference, head to Jazz Attack. Every Thursday night, this all-volunteer organization hosts a dance at the Ethical Society that begins with an hour of lessons for beginners and near beginners. You don't need a partner or any special skills to enjoy these community events, but it's advised to pre-register for entry.

Most dances are DJed events and draw crowds of around 50–70 guests. Jazz Attack provides a live band monthly, usually on the second Thursday of the month, and these occasions draw upwards of 100+ dancers to the hall. Volunteer president, Nick Cruickshank, says most people don't realize Philly is a dance hub packed with groups like this. Jazz Attack puts particular emphasis on honoring Lindy Hop's cultural roots, which differ from the mainstream idea of swing dancing popularized by white Hollywood over the decades. This is an all-welcoming space for safe expression and celebration.

In an age where no one really grows up learning to swing dance anymore, don't forget that virtually everyone comes later in life to Lindy Hop today. So there's no wrong age to drop in for the first time and learn the basics. Cruickshank says he's lost track of the number of times newcomers found their friend group, business connections, or even romantic partners within the community. It's also an energizing night out for the casually curious or even for friends just looking for something unique to do on a Thursday night.

Lindy Hop is a more improvisational style that doesn't demand mastery of any specific steps. You may want to focus on learning swing's most recognizable move, the swing out, where one partner spins into the other's arms and all the way back out again!

Address 1906 Rittenhouse Square, Philadelphia, PA 19103, www.jazzattackswings.com, jazzattackswings@gmail.com | **Getting there** Bus 12 to Rittenhouse Square & 19th Street | **Hours** Thu 8–11pm | **Tip** *American Bandstand* was filmed in West Philadelphia for the first seven years of its wildly popular run at what is now the Enterprise Center. A historical marker here tells the story (4548 Market Street).

54 Jim Loewer Glass

Blow your own masterpiece

You can purchase glass pieces by Jim Loewer in more than 200 locations in nearly 40 states and even worldwide, but only in Philadelphia can you regularly see the artist himself in action – and even learn from him. While you'll find Loewer glass in museum gift shops from the Philadelphia Museum of Art to the Smithsonian American Art Museum in the capital, the hometown artist's eye-catching works are designed to be loved and used in the everyday home. With vibrant colors and whimsical designs, bowls, tumblers, sun catchers, vases, ornaments, and more are produced in the city's Hawthorne neighborhood, with reasonable prices making the utilitarian art more widely accessible than it looks.

Still, while the Philly studio is a worthwhile retail therapy locale and equally inspiring as a window-shopping destination, the chief benefit of having this renowned artist calling Philadelphia home is the ability to learn from Loewer directly. People of all skill levels are welcome at the studio. If you're a bit of the socially anxious sort who spends too much mental space comparing your progress to that of others, opt for private lessons with one-on-one instruction that decreases in cost as your skill level grows. If, however, you're a social learner, book a party for a group lesson on blowing pendants or other small trinkets with your most creative friends, or sign up for a slot in a group class learning the art of paperweights, animals, and other specific shapes.

Should you fall in love with the torch, Loewer can customize lesson packages to your unique skills and goals as you expand your glass blowing repertoire.

Ultimately, you don't need to have an artistic bone in your body to enjoy a class at Jim Loewer Glass. If marveling is more your speed, book a demonstration to sit back and watch the master at work while he explains advanced techniques – it's BYOB.

Address 1241 Carpenter Street, Philadelphia, PA 19147, +1 (267) 243-5843, www.loewerglass.com, jimloewer@gmail.com | Getting there Bus 45 to 12th & Carpenter Streets | Hours Thu–Tue 9am–9pm, Wed 9am–5pm, see website for class schedule | Tip The Woodmere Art Museum focuses on Delaware Valley artists, including Jim Loewer (9201 Germantown Avenue, www.woodmereartmuseum.org).

55 John E. Freyer Marker

A small testament to a monumental shift

With a prominent gayborhood including rainbow crosswalks and street signs, Philly is one of the most LGBTQIA+-friendly cities in the country, but it wasn't always this way. In the early 1970s, homosexuality was still classified as a mental illness by the American Psychiatric Association (APA). Suggested cures included lobotomy and electroshock treatment, and being a homosexual was a firing offense nationwide. From these social, medical, and legal norms not even Philadelphia was immune. But one brave Philadelphian stood up to the establishment and instigated a major societal shift with one daring speech.

In 1972, closeted gay psychiatrist John E. Freyer joined a panel at the annual APA meeting to declare that he did not believe homosexuality was a "sociopathic personality disturbance," as the APA officially labeled it. The real problem, he continued, was a pervasive societal disease of homophobia. As an untenured professor at Temple University School of Medicine, Freyer put his job and reputation at serious risk by placing himself in the national spotlight, so he spoke under the pseudonym of Dr. H. Anonymous, wearing a disguise of a rubber mask and wig with a baggy suit and speaking through a voice modifying microphone. His passionate appearance on the panel succeeded in prompting the APA to launch a committee investigating their designation. The following year, homosexuality was declassified as a mental illness in the APA's Diagnostic and Statistical Manual, still used by all American psychiatric professionals for diagnoses today.

Freyer didn't officially reveal his identity until the 1994 meeting of the APA, and he spent the later years of his career treating gay men with AIDS before passing in 2003. In 2017, the Historical Society of Pennsylvania installed this marker to honor the Philadelphian's monumental contribution toward destigmatizing homosexuality nationwide.

Address 13th & Locust Street, Philadelphia, PA 19107, +1 (215) 732-6200, www.hsp.org | **Getting there** Light Rail to 12/13th & Locust Street (PATCO Line); Subway to Walnut–Locust (Broad Street Line) | **Hours** Daily accessible 24 hours | **Tip** The Historical Society of Pennsylvania is located across the street from this marker. It contains 217 boxes of Freyer's personal papers, available to the public (1300 Locust Street, www.hsp.org).

56 King's Highway Bridge
Built for Penn, used by Washington

When William Penn built his mansion on the opposite side of Pennypack Creek from Philadelphia proper, he found himself considerably inconvenienced going to and from the city. The most influential person in the colony, he asked the city to build him a bridge, and they complied. In 1697, the construction of King's Highway Bridge made Penn's work commute easier, and this stone perk of power remains standing today, continuously in use for more than 300 years as the nation's oldest road bridge.

While it truly is accurate to say the bridge was built for Penn's convenience, it also happened to be located on the most important road in the colonies, King's Highway, which connected Charleston, South Carolina, to Boston, Massachusetts. Though the full road wasn't completed until 1735, it began as early as 1650 and was well underway when Penn requested his bridge. In 1683, Pennsylvania passed a law requiring citizens to build bridges over all waterways along the growing Kings Highway, so it likely wasn't too difficult for Penn to convince his neighbors to choose a site particularly beneficial to his own needs, as a bridge was mandated in the vicinity regardless.

For decades, anyone traveling to Philadelphia from the North needed to cross this bridge, and that included the Continental Army on its way to winning the decisive Battle of Yorktown, as well as George Washington on his way to his first presidential inauguration. As we've progressed from carriages to cars, the bridge has seen plenty of upgrades and reinforcements over the centuries and was even a toll bridge for almost all of the 19th century. Its addition to the National Register of Historic Places in 1988 assures its historical integrity will remain intact for your own trip across the bridge, and for long after. Today, it's better known as either the Frankford Avenue Bridge or the Pennypack Creek Bridge.

Address 8300 Frankford Avenue, Philadelphia, PA 19136 | Getting there Bus 66 to Frankford & Solly Avenues | Hours Unrestricted | Tip Just beyond the bridge, you'll find Pennypack Trail, perfect for wooded walks through Pennypack Park. Take the trail north from Frankford (Frankford Avenue & Ashburner Street, www.phila.gov).

57_LGBT Community Center

A local resource of national proportion

William Way LGBT Community Center has been a resource hub and support group for Philadelphia's LGBTQIA+ community since it was first established as a not-for-profit in 1976, though it bore a couple different names and has had a few address changes (and even a stint of homelessness) through the years. In 1997, the organization purchased its current building on Spruce Street and hired its first executive director, kicking off a period of growth and stability that continues today.

The center is named for late city planner and activist William "Bill" Way, who held meetings in his living room for the four years the organization had no physical address. It offers counseling, employment resources, recovery meetings, wellness programs, and more for residents, but there's plenty for you to experience outside of meetings and need-specific programs.

The Community Center's large lending library contains more than 14,000 LGBTQIA+-related volumes, and you don't need to be a member to check them out. In fact, you don't even need to check them out at all. You're free to browse one of the largest collections of LGBTQIA+ works in the country and read the books onsite – a great rainy day activity!

Most intriguing are the John J. Wilcox, Jr. Archives, containing decades of personal and business files pertaining to area LGBTQIA+ history, along with preserved collections of photos, zines, albums, newspaper clippings, and objects that tell the personal stories of the community in Philadelphia and Delaware Valley. The nationally-renowned archives are open to all – just fill out a form, and you're good to go.

Even if you don't have the time or interest in reading and researching the day away, you can drop by the center's Art Gallery (it's the lobby) for local art shows. Additional special exhibitions in the Archive's Gallery highlight themed items from the massive collection.

Address 1315 Spruce Street, Philadelphia, PA 19107, +1 (215) 732-2220, www.waygay.org, info@waygay.org | Getting there Light Rail to 12/13th & Locust Streets (PATCO Line); Bus 12, 42 to Walnut & 13th Streets | Hours See website for hours and events schedule | Tip Just outside, turn down narrow Juniper Street to view the block-long mural, *Pride and Progress*, depicting a Philadelphia gay pride festival (1315 Spruce Street, www.muralarts.org).

58 Lydia Darrah School

Moderne building honoring a Revolutionary spy

If you're not familiar with Style Moderne architecture, don't fret – you're in the majority, and you probably know more about it than you think. Gaining popularity in the second half of the 1920s, it has all the same Art Deco emphases on geometric design and movement evoked by long lines but focuses on the horizontal, in contrast to Deco's vertical fascination. The two styles are often conflated, as Art Deco has remained popular in the century since its inception, while Style Moderne has nearly disappeared. In the Francisville neighborhood of Philadelphia, though, you'll find a striking example of this overlooked style, and it's named for an equally undersung Revolutionary War spy.

As Betsy Ross (see ch. 64) remains a household name for her alleged contributions to the cause, Lydia Darragh's fame is far less universal, even in her home city (though the veracity of their tales is about equal). While Ross is renowned for her morale-boosting sewing skills, Darragh's tale is one of espionage that saved the Continental Army. Publicly pacifist, her Quaker family remained in Philly when more than half the population fled during the British occupation. In reality, she was pro-Revolution and used her proximity to spy on the British. As luck would have it, General Howe eventually occupied her own house *and* let her family stay. Legend holds that Darragh hid in a closet as Howe planned a surprise attack on Washington's troops at Whitemarsh. She then got word to the general and ultimately saved the army.

Today, the Lydia Darrah School building (missing the g) stands as a memorial to both Darragh and the rare style it exemplifies with its fluted columns and long, rectangular form. The façade's ornate trim of colorful terracotta tiles is the building's eye-catching highlight, but don't expect to get inside anymore, unless you know someone renting one of the converted apartments within.

Address 718 N 17th Street, Philadelphia, PA 19130 | Getting there Subway to Fairmount Avenue (Broad Street Line) | Hours Viewable from the outside only | Tip Lydia Darragh was buried at Friends Arch Street Meetinghouse Burial Ground, now covered by buildings and parking lots. You can visit the historical marker, if not her specific grave (Arch & 3rd Streets, www.historicasmh.org).

59 Magic Gardens
There's a secret among the murals

It's difficult to walk around Philadelphia without stumbling upon one of the colorful and often shimmering mosaics of Isaiah Zagar. After all, the city's walls are home to more than 220 of these whimsical works, from small pieces in quiet alleys to full-wall takeovers on major streets. And you've almost definitely seen the vast collection on South Street, where non-profit Philadelphia's Magic Gardens now hosts both an outdoor sculpture labyrinth and indoor galleries.

Decorating Philly for decades, Zagar's works have possibly been a part of your Philly life as long as you can remember, and you may have spotted countless curious details within them over the years. But did you know that many of them contain self-portraits?

Self-identifying with Shiva, the Hindu god of both destruction and transformation, a pair of concepts all too familiar to the artist, who must shatter other works in order to create his own, Zagar has depicted himself throughout his mosaics as a man with three arms on one side and one on the other. His self-portraits take on an added layer of meaning when he describes the speed of his output, joking that if you photographed him while working, he would appear to have many arms. While Zagar was instrumental in founding Philadelphia's Magic Gardens and is still creating new art today, the octogenarian is no longer directly involved with the organization, serving as an occasional consultant and providing the stories and histories of his work for posterity.

You can take a self-guided city tour of Zagar's murals with an interactive map available on the organization's website, or you can visit the Magic Gardens directly for an immersive experience and more detailed background. Either way, keep an eye out for the artist's self-portraits wherever you spot the mosaics from now on. Zagar may be the most artistically represented modern man in Philadelphia.

Address 1020 South Street, Philadelphia, PA 19147, +1 (215) 733-0390, www.phillymagicgardens.org, info@phillymagicgardens.org | **Getting there** Bus 45 to 11th & South Streets | **Hours** Wed–Mon 11am–6pm | **Tip** You can also appreciate the equally impressive mosaics of artist Joyce Kozloff, which are more traditional in representational form, within the lobby of One Penn Center (1617 John F Kennedy Boulevard, www.associationforpublicart.org).

60 Maillardet's Automaton
The future, according to the past

Long before robots assisted in surgical operations, worked on assembly lines, or vacuumed our floors, at least one machine was impressing the literati with its astounding ability to write three complete poems and replicate four drawings – in the 18th century!

The mysteries surrounding the humanoid automaton have been many through the centuries, though most have been resolved today. It's believed to have the largest memory of any such machine in history, and it's only through its own memory that we have any idea what it even is. After a Franklin Institute machinist managed to repair the nearly destroyed donation to working order, it proceeded to produce its art and, when complete, signed the works with the line "Written by the Automaton of Maillardet," in French.

A victim of fire, the automaton's original outfit and gender remained unknown for years, and it donned a dress and a Red Cross uniform over time. In 1826, a photograph revealed it was originally a boy. Today, it's displayed without costume to show its intricate mechanical workings, serving as the centerpiece of the Institute's *Amazing Machine* exhibit.

That the institute's experts have been able to restore the automaton to such a degree of functionality without any blueprints or even knowledge of its origin (initially) is astounding alone, but the current team is convinced its head and eye movements were even more human, and they continue to seek improvements to these motions. Any more lifelike, and the automaton might be more frightening than awe-inspiring.

Still, Assistant Director of Collections Susannah Carroll insists, "When he looks up at you after finishing a piece, it feels like he is really looking at you and would welcome your praise." Speaking of inspiration, Carroll also says this mechanical wonder inspired Brian Selznick's *The Invention of Hugo Cabret*, which was made into the 2011 film *Hugo*.

Address 222 N 20th Street, Philadelphia, PA 19103, +1 (215) 448-1200, www.fi.edu, guestservices@fi.edu | Getting there Bus 7, 48, 49 to 21st & Winter Streets FS | Hours Daily 9:30am–5pm | Tip Go treasure hunting at Anastacia's Antiques, where maybe you'll find a unique humanoid of your own to bring home (617 Bainbridge Street, www.anastaciasantiques.com).

61 Manayunk Canal Towpath

Recreation among the remnants of industry

Greater Philadelphia is home to more than 300 miles of connected trails known as "The Circuit," a project that will ultimately comprise over 800 miles as the region's other trails are progressively connected. All of these off-road pathways are at least 10 feet wide, paved, and accessible to both pedestrians and bicyclists, offering outdoor recreation and healthier commuting opportunities throughout the city and its surroundings. But one of the most intriguing stretches lies behind Main Street in Manayunk.

Adjacent to the canal, the Manayunk Canal Towpath was once trodden by donkeys pulling coal-laden barges during the neighborhood's industrial heyday. Today, it's a picturesque pathway among the remnants of 19th-century commerce. Along the roughly two miles of pathway, you'll encounter defunct textile mills, original canal locks dating back more than two centuries, the locktender's house ruins, and the canal's sluice house in an impressive stretch of abandoned history. But you won't be expected to identify these structures on your own, as historical markers provide plenty of intel along the route, detailing Manayunk's rich canal heritage.

As the neighborhood continues its revitalization, an increasing number of these historical buildings are restored and converted into trendy restaurants and modern housing. The vibe continues to evolve from neglected to respected, with murals and other public art pieces along the route. On your first visit, take a leisurely stroll for the opportunity to read the signage and properly appreciate the local art. But consider biking during future visits, especially if you plan to continue onward along the rest of the 30-mile Schuylkill River Trail, of which the Towpath is just one small piece. You can rent a bicycle in Manayunk if you don't have one or don't live nearby.

Address Lock Street & Main Street, Philadelphia, PA 19127, +1 (215) 482-9565, www.manayunk.com, info@manayunk.org | Getting there Light Rail to Manayunk (Manayunk/Norristown Line); Bus 36, 61, 62 to Main & Pensdale Streets | Hours Unrestricted | Tip The arch bridge over the Towpath is part of the Manayunk Bridge Trail, offering additional river and downtown views (Dupont & High Streets, www.circuittrails.org/find-trails/manayunk-bridge-trail).

62 Mask and Wig Clubhouse
A long tradition of musical-comedy wit and whimsy

It's easy to imagine that Philadelphia would have a weak theater scene with nearby New York City scooping up actors, playwrights, and investors. But that's hardly the case. Where less scrappy cities might wither in the shadow of Broadway's monumental presence, Philadelphia shines, enticing talent *away* from New York City for its own culture-loving citizens.

There are plenty of big-name theaters around town, but performances from a number of the city's university clubs are equally worth experiencing. One of them holds the distinction of being the oldest all-male collegiate musical comedy troupe in the nation.

That's a fairly specific claim to fame indeed, but the Mask and Wig Club of University of Pennsylvania has been producing shows in Philadelphia for more than 120 years. It reached soaring heights in the mid-20th century, creating original songs covered by Ella Fitzgerald, Benny Goodman, and Tommy Dorsey. And it's not just the writing that made waves through the years. The club's performance *Joan of Arkansas* was the world's first-ever electrically recorded album (1925).

During these years of fabulous fame, the club traveled the nation annually in its own private Pennsylvania Railroad car, taking its original shows on the road. This tradition continues at alumni clubs across the world, albeit without the private rail car.

Today, the Mask and Wig Clubhouse is on the National Register of Historic Places, and the ambiance remains largely unchanged from its 19th-century beginnings, though facilities have been significantly upgraded with air conditioning and features for full accessibility. The club produces three shows per year, but the original "Annual Production," performed January through April, is the main event, and it's the only one performed at the historic Clubhouse. You can also rent the sizable Clubhouse venue for events year-round.

Address 310 S Quince Street, Philadelphia, PA 19107, +1 (215) 716-7378, www.maskandwig.com | **Getting there** Light Rail to 9–10th & Locust (PATCO Line); Bus 45 to 12th & Spruce Streets | **Hours** See website for schedule | **Tip** The University of Pennsylvania Museum was designed by the same famed local architect, Wilson Eyre (3260 Spruce Street, www.penn.museum).

63 Mount Moriah Cemetery

Is Betsy Ross still in this unowned cemetery?

When the last officer of the Mount Moriah Cemetery Association died in 2004, no one was left behind to care for – or about – the 154-year-old cemetery on the southwest border of Philadelphia. Nobody informed the city that the unowned cemetery had gone defunct until news reports in 2011 advertised its total neglect, putting the final nail in the cemetery's coffin and bringing a public closure to the 200-acre resting place for an estimated 80,000 bodies.

It doesn't take nature long to reclaim untrodden space, and the Victorian-era cemetery was quickly overgrown by enthusiastic vines, trees, and tenacious weeds that created a spectacularly spooky and intriguing scene throughout the sprawling landscape, drawing photographers, urban explorers, and the morbidly curious. The growing attention to the abandoned space ultimately inspired the creation of the Friends of Mount Moriah Cemetery as a non-profit seeking to clear and restore the grounds, as well as digitize the historic records once belonging to the original association. Within eight years of almost exclusively volunteer efforts, roughly 50 percent of the massive property had been cleared and made safe for visitors to the beguiling cemetery.

Mount Moriah remains the largest cemetery in the state of Pennsylvania, and burials within include veterans from the American Revolutionary War through the Vietnam War, along with notable mayors, singers, actors, athletes, mobsters, diplomats, senators, inventors, and even, for a time, apocryphal seamstress of America's first flag, Betsy Ross, whose bones may or may not have been removed in 1975.

The original design and gothic statuary alone are worth exploring for both the fascinated and the casually curious alike. The sheer size of the cemetery and scale of the enormous restoration project means thousands of gravesites will remain evocatively unkempt for years to come.

Address 6201 Kingsessing Avenue, Philadelphia, PA 19142, www.friendsofmountmoriahcemetery.org, info@fommci.org | **Getting there** Light Rail to Kingsessing & Cemetery Avenues (Line 13) | **Hours** Unrestricted | **Tip** To check out the official tomb of Betsy Ross, head to the Betsy Ross House, where bones from the Mount Moriah family plot were taken. No one is completely sure whose bones they are, though (239 Arch Street, www.historicphiladelphia.org).

64_ Mummers Museum

Your chance to be a Mummer, if only for a moment

Philadelphia's Mummers Parade is the oldest folk parade in the nation. Though the traditions of mummery date back to the earliest days of the colonies, and even farther back in Europe, the first official and *legal* Mummers Parade was held in 1901. The Mummers are renowned throughout the Philadelphia region for their ostentatious outfits, incredible musicianship, and cheeky jokes, but many local residents are unaware that most of the country has never heard of a Mummer – a baffling revelation for any Philadelphian who spends all of New Year's Day nursing a hangover while watching the almost endless parade of performances. And we've all wanted to try on those costumes, whether we'd admit that publicly or not. At the Mummers Museum, a surprisingly under-visited facility, you can.

Since 1976, the Mummers Museum has been sharing the history of the parade and its clubs right in the neighborhood where many Mummers live. The space is fairly small, and it admittedly hasn't been updated much since inception, but neither have the Mummers themselves. Despite the soaring costs of costuming, sets, and club obligations, the parade is still reminiscent of its working-class origins, and so it's fitting that this free museum is not the shiniest (though some of its contents certainly are).

There's not much to be found on the first floor, but this is the only space updated annually, showcasing the Winner's Circle costumes of current champions and a video of the year's top string band performances. The real fun is upstairs, though, where you can learn the Mummers Strut and compose your own medley from the sound wall as you work your way through the truly impressive amount of history delivered throughout the space. But the highlight for any Philadelphian who's grown up watching the Mummers is found among the authentic Mummers costumes that are yours for the trying – and photographing.

Address 1100 S 2nd Street, Philadelphia, PA 19147, +1 (215) 336-3050, www.mummersmuseum.com, info@mummersmuseum.com | Getting there Bus 64 to Washington Avenue & 2nd Street | Hours Wed–Sat 9:30am–4pm | Tip The String Band Division is a parade highlight, and no one knows these instruments better than the experts at Vintage Instruments. Come in to learn, or just poke around (507 S Broad Street, www.vintage-instruments.com).

65__Neon Museum

Representing the "Workshop of the World"

Philadelphia was once an American hub of neon sign manufacturing. In the 1950s–1960s, the medium's heyday, Philly was home to more than 40 shops producing these eye-catching advertisements. Len Davidson's Neon Museum is devoted to collecting and preserving this rich heritage in the city dubbed "Workshop of the World" in a book of the same name.

Today, neon isn't used nearly as prolifically as in the past, when brands in industries like paint, ice cream, and beverages would supply their vendors with small neon signs to advertise in their windows. Davidson believes neon's modern appeal isn't just due to the bright colors or delicate craftsmanship, but the nostalgia that harkens back to a time of local commerce before Amazon and big-box stores, when shopkeepers held deep connections with their communities. The Neon Museum has amassed more than 150 of these handmade works, with visitor favorites often including the animated signs, like a man donning a toupee, a dancing Elvis, and a running greyhound. However, the giant neon crown that once adorned Pat's King of Steaks may be the locally favored *crown* jewel of the collection. It's this kind of city heritage that really drives Davidson to continue preserving Philly's neon.

Many of the pieces here are familiar to Philadelphia's older residents, and the museum collects their stories as they visit. Some memories are added to the displays' guide cards, while others are left behind on cork boards around the museum. All are lovingly amassed as the repository of local oral history grows. In addition to displaying the city's colorful heritage, the museum offers design classes and neon demonstrations, arranges themed group tours, and even allows locals to contribute to, and occasionally curate, special exhibits there. For a truly memorable backdrop, you can even rent the space for photoshoots or special events.

KELLER
RECORD SHOP
RCA VICTOR

Chez Vous Room

RILEY PIANOS

Michael's

VIDEO

SCHOOL
HOUSE
ROCK LIVE!

Menopause

The Musical

Address 1800 N American Street, Unit E, Philadelphia, PA 19122, +1 (267) 534-3883, www.neonmuseumofphiladelphia.com, info@neonmuseumofphiladelphia.com | **Getting there** Bus 57 to American & Berks Streets | **Hours** See website for hours | **Tip** The Electric Street is a public installation using Flexineon LED lighting, and it's a pretty cool walking experience with an effect quite like actual neon (1300 S Percy Street, www.percystreetproject.org).

66_Octavius V. Catto Memorial

Enormous impact from a short life

While Octavius V. Catto was many things to 19th-century Philadelphia, including athlete, civil rights activist, and educator, the location of his bronze and granite memorial at City Hall inspired artist Branly Cadet to highlight his sizable political influence, both locally and nationally, much of which was largely forgotten for nearly 150 years until this installation was unveiled in 2017. The centerpiece of the memorial is a 12-foot bronze statue of Catto leaning forward in stride toward a granite representation of a 19th-century ballot box, highlighting perhaps his greatest triumph and his ultimate tragedy in a single moment. Catto successfully fought to ratify the 15th Amendment to ban racial discrimination in voting. But on election day of 1871, the first day a Black man could legally vote, he was assassinated on his way to the ballot box.

Behind the statue, five granite pillars symbolizing an 1860s streetcar represent Catto's work to end segregation on Philadelphia's public trolleys. Each is adorned with bronze plaques and engravings that highlight his passionate advocacy and considerable impact on the city.

While his athleticism is not the primary focus of the memorial, Catto was also an accomplished sportsman, who helped establish Philadelphia as a hub of the future Negro leagues of baseball. He was a member of the Franklin Institute (see ch. 61), and a known academic and public speaker throughout Philadelphia. Despite a list of accolades and accomplishments befitting a long life, Octavius Valentine Catto was only 32 years old when Frank Kelly, a white man, shot him in front of his house in an effort to intimidate and suppress Black voters.

The Catto Memorial, officially entitled *A Quest for Parity*, finally brought this important figure back into the public consciousness. It is also the first public monument to a single Black person in the city's history.

Address S Penn Square, Philadelphia, PA 19107, +1 (215) 546-7550, www.associationforpublicart.org, apa@associationforpublicart.org | Getting there Bus 16, 27, 31, 32, BSO to Broad Street & South Penn Square | Hours Unrestricted | Tip Visit Catto's grave about 30 minutes outside the city at Eden Cemetery in Collingdale, as well as that of John Pierre Burr, abolitionist and illegitimate son of Aaron Burr (1434 Springfield Road, Collingdale, www.edencemetery.org).

67 Ohio State House

The last state house from the first World's Fair

There's a lot to unpack here, so we'll start from the top. The first World's Fair hosted in the United States was held in Philadelphia to honor the 1876 centennial of the signing of the Declaration of Independence. While some of us may recall the bicentennial celebrations of 1976, some remnants of which can still be found around Philadelphia today, none of us was present for the centennial, and very little of this celebration remains. By the fair's kickoff, 37 states had made their way into the Union (Colorado would join *during* the fair's run, becoming the 38th state in August, 1876), but of the states and countries that built exhibition houses for the world to witness, only Ohio's remains today, still standing in Fairmount Park.

Aside from Memorial Hall, now home to the Please Touch Museum and two restrooms, the Ohio State House isn't just the only centennial state house remaining, it's the only centennial building remaining, period. Constructed of Ohio's natural resources, primarily multiple varieties of sandstone (whose manufacturers were carefully labeled to advertise to interested parties), the Ohio State House was restored for the bicentennial celebrations and underwent even greater restoration before reopening to the public in 2007. The uses of the house have varied from public offices to a café briefly renowned for its oatmeal (not a claim many eateries can make). It is now home to the Fairmount Park Conservancy and protected on the Philadelphia Register of Historic Places.

Ten million people descended upon Philadelphia for the Centennial International Exhibition, the equivalent of more than one third of the entire United States population at the time, and, while Ohio may be the punchline of many a Pennsylvania joke, some respect and admiration are surely due to the only state whose house remains from this spectacular fair nearly 150 years ago.

Address 4700 States Drive, Philadelphia, PA 19131, +1 (215) 988-9334, www.myphillypark.org | **Getting there** Bus 38 to Belmont Avenue & Montgomery Drive | **Hours** Viewable from the outside only | **Tip** The other remaining building, now the Please Touch Museum since the bicentennial of 1976, is an interactive children's museum focused on the seven-and-under crowd (4231 Avenue of the Republic, www.pleasetouchmuseum.org).

68_Old St. Joseph's Church

A hidden church, then and now

To say anti-Catholic sentiment was strong in the colonies would be an understatement. Despite the notion of the United States being founded on religious freedoms, early American Protestants were vehemently, and often violently, anti-Catholic throughout the colonies, and that included Philadelphia. Thanks to William Penn's Quaker-inspired prototype to a state constitution, though, practicing Catholicism was deemed permissible in early Pennsylvania. While this may not seem like much, it's more than most colonies allowed. By the 18th century, Catholic worship was banned by British law throughout the colonies, but Philadelphia's first Catholic church was founded in 1733, nonetheless, and Old St. Joseph's remains in its original location today, despite the legal and physical attacks that ensued since.

Old St. Joseph's Church has been rebuilt twice. The current building was dedicated in 1839, and its location is a visual reminder of how dangerous it was to be Catholic in the 18th century. If you try looking for this church from a major street, you won't find it. Entrance is only granted through a gated arch in an alleyway, and legend holds that Benjamin Franklin advised this discretion to keep the building safe from attack, a fate realized at least two times when Quakers helped defend the building in 1740 and 1755.

Undaunted, Old St. Joseph's has continued regular worship through the current day, even receiving visits from early notables like the Marquis de Lafayette and the public support of George Washington and John Adams. Still, even the building's current exterior is somewhat ambiguous and unremarkable, better befitting its historic parishioners of lesser renown but perhaps greater importance, as the church racially integrated as early as the 1790s and founded an orphanage to house children left behind when Yellow Fever killed a tenth of the city in 1793.

Address 321 Willings Alley, Philadelphia, PA 19106, +1 (215) 923-1733, www.oldstjoseph.org, office@oldstjoseph.org | Getting there Bus 52 to 4th & Locust Streets | Hours Mon–Fri 11am–3pm, Sat 5–7pm, Sun 7am–1pm | Tip Around the corner, the cemetery of Old St. Mary's Church, the city's second Catholic church, contains the graves of historic residents, like Commodore Barry and several members of the Meade family (252 S 4th Street, www.oldstmary.com).

69_ Oneida Debate

Two revolutions in one

Who are the heroes of the American Revolutionary War? No matter whom you just envisioned, it's unlikely you pictured any Native Americans. At the Museum of the American Revolution you'll encounter the story of the Oneida Nation, the only Native American allies of the Continental Army.

Despite having their contributions to the colonial effort largely ignored outside of this exhibition, the Oneida weren't just the only Native American allies to the cause, they were one of the very first groups to align with colonial rebels at all, bringing intelligence and manpower to a fledgling effort desperately in need of support. In order to accomplish this, the Oneida first had to break with the Iroquois Confederacy, and this decision was not taken lightly. At the museum's Oneida Nation Theater, six lifelike replicas of Oneida members, each representing an actual person with historically accurate costume and appearance, reenact the momentous debate and decision regularly, and you're free to walk among them as you listen to their concerns and read more about their biographies.

The theater was made possible by a $10 million donation by the Oneida Indian Nation, eager to share the story of their contribution to the war effort (incidentally, the Oneida have fought with American soldiers in every conflict since, too), and the sculptural figures were crafted by a studio that has produced performance pieces for clients as high-profile as Lady Gaga. So expect some serious quality here.

Supplementing the exhibit, the museum airs a 25-minute documentary daily, detailing Oneida solidarity with the rebel cause and also acknowledging the steady land appropriation they suffered at the hands of the newly formed nation. Be sure to check back in October, too, when the museum hosts an annual Indigenous Peoples Weekend with discussions, demonstrations, performances, and more.

Address 101 S 3rd Street, Philadelphia, PA 19106, +1 (215) 253-6731, www.amrevmuseum.org | **Getting there** Bus 21, 42 to Chestnut & 3rd Streets | **Hours** Daily 10am–5pm | **Tip** Philadelphia is woefully short in representation of any of its Native American heritage. One rare example is the statue, near Penn's Landing, of Lenni-Lenape Chief Tamanend, who signed the Peace Treaty with William Penn (2 N Front Street, www.associationforpublicart.org).

70_ Original Pumpkin Spice

Philly was into pumpkin spice before it was basic

Say "pumpkin spice" to just about anyone, and you'll elicit laughs, groans, gasps, or all three. The blend has morphed from pie flavor to all-out lifestyle since a certain Seattle-based coffee company made the term practically synonymous with the entire autumn season through the unprecedented success of its now-signature latte. But long before pumpkin spice became the hallmark of the "Basic" lifestyle, a label plenty of people adopt proudly, and ages before it spread to products in every aisle of the supermarket (including cleaning products), Philadelphia had the spiced wafer.

Spiced wafers are perhaps best described as amped-up gingersnaps, with many of the same ingredients plus a few more spices. And the original brand, Sweetzels, comes in a distinctive orange and black box that dominates grocery store displays each fall. What many Philadelphians don't know, though, is that these cookies are *only* here. Though they seem as natural here as cheesesteaks and soft pretzels, the rest of the country, for the most part, simply doesn't yet have this Philly tradition that has tantalized generations for more than 100 years.

In fact, when a local grocery chain expanded a bit too far out of the region and set up their spiced wafer display after Labor Day, they were stunned to find no one was buying them. As it turned out, their sales would reveal that there's a fairly firm 60-mile radius from Philadelphia where people purchase these beloved autumnal treats, and it's difficult to get anyone beyond that boundary even to notice them. That's just fine with Philly.

At The Dining Car in Northeast Philly, you can get your *original* pumpkin spice fix seasonally with the diner's sell-out Sweetzels Shake, combining vanilla ice cream with crumbles of the beloved cookie. If this crowd favorite seems a tad too juvenile for you, ask about the adults-only version, spiked with spiced rum.

Address 8826 Frankford Avenue, Philadelphia, PA 19136, +1 (215) 338-5113, www.thediningcar.com | Getting there Bus 66, 68 to Frankford Avenue & Placid Street | Hours Daily 7:30am – 2:30pm | Tip Looking for uniquely Philly bites outside of autumn? Try the Pennsylvania General Store in Reading Terminal Market, where the name of the game is PA-made (1136 Arch Street, www.pageneralstore.com).

71 Painted Bride

Incubating a city's underserved communities

When Painted Bride realized too many of its resources were tied up in its physical space, it untethered itself from its address. The primary focus of Painted Bride is to foster artists and leaders among lower-income communities of color, and the organization didn't find owning expensive real estate in a gentrified community to be contributing to that mission. So it sold the building. Today, the organization works directly in the communities it seeks to nurture. You might assume that public engagement with Painted Bride would have dropped. But the opposite is true.

While you may not always see the organization's face at events, its cultivation and support of artists and creative leaders around the city are providing the resources necessary for *them* to produce community events, exhibitions, and programs, and their newfound flexibility brings these opportunities directly to your neighborhood.

With a calendar now populated by events like the drag-hosted *Off the Wall* exhibit, bringing art to people traditionally excluded from galleries to create "human connection and radical joy," and a series of community pot-luck picnic art shows, Painted Bride pop-ups are now limited only by the community's imagination. And yes, it also still commissions and supports performances of dance, poetry, and other more easily-defined genres, too.

You can also get actively involved even if you're not a creative. Many Bride-sponsored programs rely on community engagement, like Power to the Prompt, which asks the public to respond to prompts and then commissions artists to represent the replies through original works. The annual Run Away with the Bride scavenger hunt is a fundraiser that will have you scouting some of the city's most culturally and artistically significant sights with friends, and it's pretty low-key as far as contests go. After all, Painted Bride is about fostering connections, not competition.

Address Various, +1 (215) 925-9914, www.paintedbride.org, info@paintedbride.org | Getting there Varies by event | Hours See website for event schedule | Tip Vox Populi is an artist collective supporting under-represented artists and hosts free public exhibitions on the first Friday of each month (319 N 11th Street, www.voxpopuligallery.org).

72 Patti LaBelle Way

A permanent home for a Philly legend

Legendary singer and two-time Grammy Award winner Patti LaBelle is a Philadelphia native, and, though she's relocated around Philly a handful of times, she now has a permanent place in her favorite city. No, it's not her *home* address, though she does still live here and claims she will not move again; it's the stretch of Broad Street, between Locust Street and Spruce Street, which was officially named Patti LaBelle Way in the summer of 2019.

LaBelle attended the unveiling ceremony and autographed a copy of the street signs that would be posted along the 200–300 block of Broad Street, honoring her legacy in her beloved city. However, there was one very noticeable difference between what was signed and what was hung. LaBelle's autographed sign was unflawed, but those that were actually hung on the street were all misspelled, failing to capitalize the "B" in the superstar's last name. Media across the country picked up on the gaffe immediately, and Philadelphia was quick to respond with properly-spelled replacements. Was LaBelle offended? If she was, she never showed it, instead offering tremendous gratitude and thanking the city for the love she felt.

LaBelle has described Philadelphia as a grounding influence that provides quiet for her soul. After loving a life of raising her family here, she is now selling Patti's Good Life products at Walmart nationwide. Despite her international success, she's always been the family chef at her Philadelphia home (among other household chores), but now we can all sample her recipes through this partnership with the mega retailer. And how good are they? A 2015 viral video review of LaBelle's sweet potato pies caused a nationwide sell-out that saw the under-$5 pies selling for upwards of $50 each on eBay. And this was no short-lived trend – in 2020, Walmart reported they were still selling the pies at a rate of 25 per minute.

Address Patti LaBelle Way, 200–299 S Broad Street, Philadelphia, PA 19102, between Spruce & Locust Streets | Getting there Bus 27, 32 to Broad & Spruce Streets | Hours Unrestricted | Tip Head to Booker's Restaurant & Bar to sample some of LaBelle's favorite Southern-influenced cooking in Philadelphia (5021 Baltimore Avenue, www.bookersrestaurantandbar.com).

73 _ Philadelphia Independents

Philly-centric, Philly-made, Philly-proud

The punny name of this Old City boutique honors both the independent makers who produce all of its goodies and the independent ownership of the shop by its three-woman team of Philly fanatics.

Everything inside Philadelphia Independents is handmade by Philly locals. The shop features the work of roughly 60 area artisans and spans from gift cards and candles to art and décor, with all manner of quirk between. And yes, the boutique's clever name also alludes to the Philly focus of many of the wares, including nods to the shop's enviable address in "America's Most Historic Square Mile." Because of its location, plenty of the clientele are travelers hunting for authentic souvenirs, but this spot is also special to savvy locals who recognize the one-of-a-kind nature of the hometown gifts within.

None of the boutique's three owners are originally from Philadelphia, but don't judge too harshly: Tiffica, Ashley, and Jennifer all came here for college and loved the city so deeply they not only stayed, but opened a store entirely devoted to it. With so much artisan commerce now relegated to the digital world, the trio noticed that the community lacked a brick-and-mortar hub for Philly artisans to share their work in a central location, despite demand from locals for a way to support these area small businesses. Now, more than ever, tourists want to support the communities they visit as well, so this all-local, all-handmade gift boutique seemed like the natural solution.

Among the hottest commodities at Philadelphia Independents? Anything Gritty. The personality-packed Flyer's mascot, who was so very bipolarizing when unveiled in 2018, is now an international superstar, and shop co-owner Ashley Peel says the "hot hockey hunk" (yes, we're talking about the same googly-eyed, orange monster) is quite popular here, gracing stickers and pins to tote bags and more.

Address 35 N 3rd Street, Philadelphia, PA 19106, +1 (267) 773-7316, www.philadelphiaindependents.com, hello@philadelphiaindependents.com | Getting there Bus 17, 33 to Market & 3rd Streets | Hours Mon–Sat 11am–7pm, Sun 11am–5pm | Tip To support another women-owned home and gift shop, check out Open House in Midtown Village (107 S 13th Street, www.openhouseliving.com).

74 Philadelphia Stars Memorial Park

A small tribute to a major contribution

On an unassuming corner across Parkside Avenue from Fairmount Park, a humble memorial hints at the greatness of the former Philadelphia Stars, whose field once stood on this site. A historical marker was added to this corner in 1998, oh-so-briefly summarizing the 85-year-history of "African American Baseball in Philadelphia." It primarily highlights the championship wins of various teams that paved the way for the Negro National League's Philadelphia Stars, but it wasn't until 2005 that most took any serious note of this historic space.

Now officially dedicated Philadelphia Stars Negro League Memorial Park, the wood-fenced area of pavers and landscaping is home to Philly artist Phil Sumpter's seven-foot bronze of a Negro Leagues baseball player, commanding attention from the center of the park. Originally cast in 2003, the statue was moved in 2005 to its permanent home here, atop a pedestal bearing the names of five former Philadelphia Stars players who were present at the dedication. Beyond the statue is a pair of low granite walls bearing the inscribed names of Philadelphia Stars players, along with those of other Negro League greats.

Take a look across Belmont Avenue at the building-wide mural depicting scenes from the 44th & Parkside Ballpark honored here today. Dedicated a year after the park, in 2006, this David McShane work was commissioned by Mural Arts Philadelphia, the largest public art program in the nation.

The success of the Negro Leagues was due in large part to Philadelphia's long tradition of supporting Black baseball, and games here would draw thousands of weekly spectators. The Philly-packed roster of the Cuban Giants in 1885 was considered the nation's first professional Black baseball team, decades before the Negro National League was formed in 1920.

Address Belmont & Parkside Avenue, Philadelphia, PA 19104, +1 (215) 546-7550, www.associationforpublicart.org, apa@associationforpublicart.org | **Getting there** Bus 40, 43, 64 to Parkside & Belmont Avenues | **Hours** Unrestricted | **Tip** The African American Museum in Philadelphia is the nation's first municipally-funded museum of African American heritage and contains some local Negro Leagues memorabilia (701 Arch Street, www.aampmuseum.org).

75 Prison Synagogue
The first in the nation

Spooky season in the tristate area surrounding Philadelphia brings to mind one very famous building, Eastern State Penitentiary. The fifteen "haunted" attractions at this long-closed state prison (it's been more than 50 years since it ceased operation) that once famously held Al Capone are renowned as the premier Halloween attraction in the region, and its neo-gothic design was intentionally chosen to instill fear. But this behemoth is better visited any time *but* October – and during the day.

Eastern State Penitentiary played a pivotal role in US criminal reform efforts as one of the first prisons to focus on rehabilitation rather than mere incarceration, and tours today end with an exhibit that brings into question the efficacy of the current prison model in the United States. At the time of its 1829 construction, this was the largest and most expensive public building in the nation. Several areas have been restored, including the hospital, operating room, kitchen, and Death Row, though no inmates were ever actually executed at Eastern State. But one of the most remarkable sites in the prison remained in ruin until 2009.

The nation's first known synagogue inside a prison was constructed here, allowing the small population of Jewish inmates to worship and celebrate freely. So freely, in fact, that this was the only religious group in the prison's history permitted to meet without a guard present. In complete ruin when located by a graduate student, the synagogue was restored to its 1959 appearance through donations and a year-long effort, complete with a flickering eternal flame.

In a former exercise yard next to the synagogue, an exhibit on Jewish life at the prison includes artifacts, like the synagogue's original painted door from 1924, left slightly ajar. You can visit the synagogue and mini museum, as they are now part of Eastern State Penitentiary's regular tour.

Address 2027 Fairmount Avenue, Philadelphia, PA 19130, +1 (215) 236-3300, www.easternstate.org | Getting there Bus 49 to Fairmount & Corinthian Avenue | Hours Tours daily 10am–5pm, seasonal twilight tours | Tip Directly outside the penitentiary, and sharing its guard walls, Eastern State Penitentiary Park reclaims some ground for the whole family with community gardens and a year-round public lawn and Playpen Playground (Brown Street & Corinthian Avenue, www.fespp.com).

76 *Pulse* Fountain

The train timetable you didn't know existed

If you've passed through Dilworth Park at night during the warmer months since 2018, you've probably noticed the seemingly random bursts of green mist that occasionally shoot up from the park's epic, 11,000-square-foot fountain of otherwise dancing jets. You may even have spotted them during the day, too, when the color is still somewhat visible, though considerably less vibrant. If you assumed they were just more fun for the kids frolicking among the fountains, you were wrong. They're part of an intricate installation from artist Janet Echelman that not only recalls area history, but provides reliable information on some of the city's public transportation.

Described by the artist as "a living x-ray of the city's circulatory system," the colored mist of *Pulse* follows the path of the trains traveling directly below – and in real time. When you see a four-foot eruption of green mist in the park, you can be sure a green line train is currently chugging along below. This track is for the subway-surface trolley lines that otherwise operate aboveground in most other parts of the city, and there are plans to illuminate both the Market Frankford-Line (blue) and Broad Street Line (orange) as funding becomes available.

Though it partially represents the steam from both the city's first water pumping station (installed here in the 19th century) and the trains of the former Pennsylvania Railroad Station across the street, Pulse does not employ steam. The cool mist is colored only by LED lighting, so it's completely harmless. You're encouraged to interact with it (particularly if you're a child, but nobody will be judging you).

Because *Pulse* tracks real train movement, the best way to ensure you're in the right place at the right time to catch sight of the mist (or snap a snazzy photo of yourself inside it) is simply to check the train schedule.

Address 1 S 15th Street, Philadelphia, PA 19102, +1 (215) 440-5500, www.centercityphila.org, info@centercityphila.org | **Getting there** Subway to 15th Street (Market–Frankford Line); Light Rail to 15th Street (10, 11, 13, 34, 36 Lines) | **Hours** Daily Apr–Oct 7:45–1am | **Tip** If you've been inspired to learn more about Philly's public transportation system, check out the free Septa Transit Museum (1234 Market Street, www.septa.org).

77 _ Quince Street
The most charming, among alleys

Long gone are the days when alleys were considered dark and dangerous. Today, they conjure notions of historic charm and quaint strolls, both of which are offered in abundance along the four blocks of quiet Quince Street. While Elfreth's Alley may be Philly's most famous, touting its claim as America's oldest continuously inhabited alley – and it truly is drenched in period splendor – you'd be remiss to overlook lesser-known Quince Street for the heavily-trafficked title holder.

Spanning from Lombard Street northward to Walnut Street, the narrow alley is a pedestrian's paradise of Center City solace and brimming with historic homes. The entire route is not long, so feel free to stretch your legs from start to finish. But pay special attention to the blocks on either side of Spruce Street for the highlights. Here is where you'll find the quaintest of Quince, flanked by brick homes subtly dressed in window box finery with striking accents of painted doors and shutters. Along your way, extend your explorations by turning down some of the side streets you'll encounter on these blocks. They're often just as fetching, and the tiny turns bring a neighborhood warmth that's a bit lacking along blockbuster Elfreth's, which is decidedly shorter.

The pinnacle of picturesque perfection is achieved with an autumn visit to Quince Street, when its ubiquitous gingko trees drop a deluge of yellow leaves that give the span a genuine streets-paved-with-gold aura guaranteed to dazzle. Still, this one's worth exploring year-round, as window boxes and stoop landscaping give way to holiday decorations in winter, and the gas-lamp romance of yesteryear carries the cobblestone street through to spring again. Regardless of timing, you'll always find the moment of respite that makes Quince Street a true treasure of tranquility amid the bustle of surrounding Center City.

Address Quince Street, Philadelphia, PA 19107 | **Getting there** Bus 45 to 12th & Streets | **Hours** Unrestricted | **Tip** If you haven't explored Elfreth's Alley yet, it's jus minutes northeast of here and well worth the stroll (Elfreth's Alley, www.elfrethsal

78 Rail Park

It's even greener than you think

Finding green space in a city is always a welcome respite and, quite literally, provides a breath of fresh air. And some spaces are greener than you may realize. Philadelphia's Rail Park is repurposing abandoned railways to transform them into public parks filled with art, gardens, native trees, and community events. It also prevented much of the contaminated soil below from being unearthed and exposed to the environment had the structures been demolished instead. It was also cheaper to renovate than demolish the largely elevated tracks and deal with contaminated waste, so with cost surely a consideration, it's an economic and an ecological win.

Encouraged by the wild success of New York City's elevated High Line, the Rail Park will ultimately bring three miles of new greenspace to Philadelphia, both above the city and below, and will end at Fairmount Park. Part of the Viaduct phase, stretching from Chinatown to Northern Liberties, has been open since 2018. At just 1,400 feet, this is the smallest segment of the park's planned phases, opened as something of a test run, and it's packed with more than a thousand plantings, a mural designed by Shepard Fairey (whose Obama portrait now hangs at the National Portrait Gallery), an electrically-equipped performance stage, and its most charming feature, a row of adult-friendly porch swings with skyline views.

Among the most fascinating finds here, though, is the 80-foot Story Wall of laser-cut steel, mapping the Rail Park and its industrial heritage, as shown in an 1895 atlas of the city. Flooding the map are images, logos, and details of the businesses that once boomed on the streets below, paying homage to Philadelphia's remarkable history of industrial prowess.

It's the remnants of that industry that physically support the park today, as nature reclaims some of its former territory with a little help from the community.

Address 1300 Noble Street, Philadelphia, PA 19123, +1 (215) 485-2221, www.therailpark.org, friends@therailpark.org | Getting there Bus 23, 61 to 11th & Noble Streets | Hours Daily 7am–10pm | Tip You can spot another Shepard Fairey mural, *Lotus Diamond*, in Fishtown (1228 Frankford Avenue, www.muralarts.org).

79 __ Random Tea Room

Shopping, sipping, and co-working in serenity

When calm and serenity are the order of the day, one of Philly's most charming spaces is the Random Tea Room in Northern Liberties. Owner Rebecca Goldschmidt opened the shop in 2008 with no prior knowledge of tea culture, but an aversion to coffee's effect on her body and a general sense that she didn't fit the coffee shop vibe.

Undaunted, she embarked on a personal journey with her tea sensei, Jor, and hired herbalists to help make the most informed choices for the shop's herbal apothecary. Today, she's well-versed in tea and continues to learn nuances from her staff and even her customers within the tea community she's helped inspire. While there's plenty here to satisfy the fussiest of tea sippers, the welcoming atmosphere and learn-as-you-go culture will put you at ease as soon as you enter, regardless of your tea experience.

Around the Random Tea Room, you'll find the works of local artists and artisans for sale, from jewelry to, of course, one-of-a-kind ceramic mugs, and regularly changing exhibitions. A visit here is as much a visual arts experience as a culinary journey, and the coziness extends outdoors to the quaint backyard garden space. Come by for an afternoon cup, or develop your home ritual with the shop's custom refillable tea station kits. You'll also find everything else you need to elevate your home tea game, including kettles, timers, and natural tea additions.

As for the tea itself, you can stock up on an impressive array of Darjeeling; oolong; black; Chinese green, white, and red; Japanese; yerba maté; and many more, including specialty house blends, which should appeal to just about any tea taster's preference. If the shop meets its goals of helping on your way toward a healthier lifestyle and a closer connection to your community, consider spending more time here by renting a co-working station for remote business or developing your writing hobby – it comes with a free cup of tea!

Address 713 N 4th Street, Philadelphia, PA 19123, +1 (215) 639-2442,
www.therandomtearoom.com, becky@therandomtearoom.com | Getting there Bus 57 to
4th Street & Fairmount Avenue | Hours Thu–Sun noon–6pm | Tip If you're inspired to
take your wellness journey further, Tula Yoga offers classes for all skill levels a few doors up
the block (737 N 4th Street, www.tulayogaphilly.com).

80__Rittenhouse Chess
Make your move, make a friend

The Rittenhouse Chess club is a relatively young group, but already it's seen hundreds of players sit at its boards since its founding in 2021. When Andrew Graham moved to Philadelphia without many local connections, he started a Facebook group for the chess club and set up his board in the park one Sunday afternoon. No one from the group came, and no one came the following Wednesday either, but a few trickled in the third time, and, by the fourth event, a small core of regulars was established, and the club was truly born. Today, there's a sizable number of regulars turning out to the weekly meetups, and they draw the attention of plenty more passersby curious to try a free game with a stranger.

There aren't many rules for the casual club. Essentially, bring a chessboard if you have one, though you don't need one. There's no playing for money. Likewise, it costs nothing to play. The club was founded as much with the goal of meeting other Philadelphians as getting in a few games, and for that it's been a wild success for Andrew and the others who routinely drop in.

Playing in public also allows the club to attract the attention of the many travelers strolling through the famous park, and that's brought special guests from around the world – as far away as Russia – to the boards. And speaking of unexpected special guests, at least two chess celebrities have stopped by unannounced, including International Grandmaster Greg Shahade and Grandmaster Timur Gareyev, who once famously played 48 simultaneous games, blindfolded.

Rittenhouse Chess is open to everyone, including complete beginners, and the convivial nature of the group means you won't be shunned if you do show up with absolutely no experience. Chess is the means, but friendship is the end, so give it a try and get to know some more of your neighbors and the fascinating people passing through Philly.

Address Rittenhouse Square, Walnut & 18th Streets, Philadelphia, PA 19103,
www.facebook.com/groups/rittenhousechess | **Getting there** Bus 12, 42 to Walnut &
18th Streets | **Hours** Wed 5:30pm, Sun noon | **Tip** *Your Move*, an oversized gaming sculpture
that includes a few chess pieces, is just a 10-minute walk from here (1401 John F Kennedy
Boulevard, www.associationforpublicart.org).

81 River Hammocks

Beach vibes at the riverfront

Hammocks are not just for lazy creekside afternoons in the country or treetop decks in the mountains, and if there's any space that can prove that in an instant, it's Spruce Street Harbor Park. Here, hammocks abound, and many are positioned directly along the Delaware River, and that's about as far as traditional hammock notions go in this colorful space. You certainly can try to relax, swinging between trees with a good book in hand, but this is more of an energizing hangout space than a peaceful retreat, especially at night.

Open seasonally as a free public space, Spruce Street Harbor Park brings the best of beach culture to the banks of the Delaware River. Please note we did say culture and not an actual beach – there's no ocean or sandy shoreline – so prepare for a boardwalk, arcade, local food vendors, and even a weekend beer garden, as well as additional bars open daily. The park packs a busy schedule of events from markets to performances, but the clear highlight of the space is its abundance of vibrant hammocks stretched among trees and perched along the river just about anywhere one will fit. At night, the trees above are lit with thousands of colorful LEDs, and the floating barge casts additional bursts of color onto the water below. It's a visual wonderland of chromatic bliss. It does tend to get quite crowded, but many don't realize that small groups can rent a riverside, outdoor lounge space, complete with dedicated hammocks, a great option for friends looking to spend an afternoon or evening hanging out together.

And, for something a little different, the floating barge here is also home to over-water hammocks suspended above the Delaware. There's no risk of tangling up and falling into the river below, as these spots resemble more of a rope-netted floor than a swinging hammock. They comfortably support up to three adults each.

Address 301 S Christopher Columbus Boulevard, Philadelphia, PA 19106,
+1 (215) 922-2386, www.delawareriverwaterfront.com, sshp@drwc.org | Getting there
Bus 25 to Columbus Boulevard & Spruce Street | Hours Seasonally, Sun–Thu 11am–11pm,
Fri & Sat 11am–midnight | Tip Want to get even closer to the water? Rent a nostalgic swan
boat from Paddle Penn's Landing and maneuver your way among the ships in the marina
(211 S Christopher Columbus Boulevard, www.phillyseaport.org/paddle).

82 The Rosenbach

A literary wonderland

If you're at all into literature, you must step into The Rosenbach. Two brothers, Dr. A.S.W. and Philip Rosenbach, amassed one of the world's preeminent collections of rare books and manuscripts during the early 20th century and became among the most celebrated names among American dealers and collectors. The brothers founded The Rosenbach Museum and Library in 1954 with their personal collections housed in the doctor's elegant 1865 townhouse. Today, the who's who of first editions and personal effects has overflowed to fill the neighboring townhouse, and an affiliation with the Free Library of Philadelphia Foundation expands the mind-blowing collection to more than 400,000 notable pieces.

A simple list of the museum's text-based treasures would fill a tome, but highlights of the highlights include first editions of *Alice in Wonderland, Don Quixote, Pilgrim's Progress,* and *Robinson Crusoe*; original manuscripts and notes of *Ulysses* and *Dracula;* letters and notations of Thomas Jefferson, Abraham Lincoln, and George Washington; 15th century manuscripts of *Canterbury Tales*; and the only known copy of Benjamin Franklin's first printing of *Poor Richard's Almanac* (1733). The list of scribes represented by manuscripts, letters, photographs, and first editions goes on to include Dickens (see ch. 16), Dickinson, Milton, Wilde, Keats, Shelley, Burns, and Blake in a virtually unending list of literary powerhouses featured both in townhouse tours and The Rosenbach's special exhibits.

Words aside, you'll also encounter the country's largest collection of miniature oil paintings, five centuries of antique furniture, and a jewelry and *vertu* collection with pieces connected to notables from Napoleon to Nebuchadnezzar. You'll be dazzled by the interior, but save time to take the air in the 1,600-square-foot garden populated by plants and flowers with distinct ties to the riches inside.

Address 2008–2010 Delancey Place, Philadelphia, PA 19103, +1 (215) 732-1600, www.rosenbach.org, info@rosenbach.org | Getting there Bus 17 to 19th & Spruce Streets | Hours Thu–Sat 10:30am–6pm, Sun 10:30am–4:30pm | Tip Two blocks north, Rittenhouse Square is packed with a fabulous collection of some of the city's most intriguing sculptures, spanning three centuries of work (210 W Rittenhouse Square, www.friendsofrittenhouse.org).

83__ The Rotunda
A literal arts sanctuary

Originally built as a worship sanctuary for the First Church of Christ Scientist in 1911, The Rotunda is worth a visit for its architectural design alone. The Beaux Arts-style building is striking for the paradoxically ornate simplicity of its commanding exterior, but the domed sanctuary within is a religious experience, faith aside. The 80-foot dome soars over a sea of gleaming pine and walnut, with a 1,500-pound Tiffany chandelier hanging at the center. Yet, despite its undeniable beauty and drama, this room is not even the most popular room in the house. In fact, it's not even considered the "main room" of what is today a haven for neighborhood arts owned by the University of Pennsylvania.

Some special events *are* held in the sanctuary throughout the year, but the smaller room beyond is what draws most visitors to The Rotunda. Here, in a space interchangeably known as the "main room" and the "back room," more than 300 arts events are offered annually, and it's impossible to summarize precisely the scope of genres and disciplines on display here.

On any given night, you might find spoken word, a Yiddish dance party, an Appalachian folk concert, a film series, dance battles, gongs, or panel discussions. The Rotunda's programming is focused on grassroots arts, so you're going to find neighborhood artists and performers in action whenever you drop in. A-list names have also been known to perform, too.

As a community-building initiative of the University of Pennsylvania, with strong educational and enrichment goals, The Rotunda is always an alcohol-free and smoke-free space, offering structured social alternatives through exposure to diverse arts and inclusive culture particularly beneficial to the city's younger residents. Most events are ticketed, and plenty come with a cost, but there's a fair share of free events presented throughout the calendar, too.

Address 4014 Walnut Street, Philadelphia, PA 19104, +1 (215) 934-3705, www.therotunda.org | **Getting there** Bus 30, 40, LUCYGR to 40th & Walnut Streets | **Hours** See website for events schedule | **Tip** University of Pennsylvania is home to the Chinese Rotunda, another impressive space that's even larger, with a 90-foot dome capping ancient Chinese art, part of the Penn Museum (3260 South Street, www.penn.museum).

84 Sedgley Woods Disc Golf
An older course for a newer sport

Of all the history that has poured out of Philadelphia, you may be least familiar with that of its disc golf legacy. While the notion of disc golf has been around since the early 20th century, it wasn't standardized until the 1970s and has only recently become so popular that you may even have heard of it!

The game is simple enough. Like golf, outdoor courses are set, but with poles instead of holes, and players throw discs instead of whacking balls with clubs. Of course, there are all manner of rules and specialty equipment for the more serious devotees of the sport, but anyone can stroll up to a course in a park (often woods) and try their hand without any preparation or training.

The Philadelphia Frisbee Club was founded the same year as the Professional Disc Golf Association, and Sedgley Woods became one of the first pole hole courses in the world shortly thereafter, with tournaments beginning in 1978. At the time, the curious "new" sport's tournaments drew live crowds and media coverage to Sedgley Woods, but it wasn't until the early 2000s that disc golf exploded in popularity across the United States. Today, there are more than 6,500 known courses listed in the PDGA directory. The sport remains accessible to most, and Sedgley Woods, despite its legacy within the sport, remains a free course, open year-round within Fairmount Park.

Feel free to bring any old recreational disc to the 27-hole course. Know that the thick-lipped ones you toss around your yard aren't ideal for serious sporting, and there are discs known as "drivers" and "putters," just like traditional golf, with a host of varieties between. To up your game, buy a disc from volunteers at the course, typically present on Thursday, Saturday, and Sunday, and feel free to ask them all your burning questions about the game or the course. Disc sales go toward course maintenance.

Address 33rd & W Oxford Streets, Philadelphia, PA 19121, www.sedgleywoods.com, friendsofsedgleywoods@gmail.com | Getting there Bus 32 to 33rd & Oxford Streets | Hours Daily dawn–dusk | Tip You can practice your traditional golf skills just a few minutes from here at Strawberry Green Driving Range (1500 N 33rd Street, www.phila.gov).

85 Sesame Place

The country's original Sesame Street theme park

Just outside of the city in Langhorne, Pennsylvania, Sesame Place was the world's first *Sesame Street* theme park when it opened in 1980. What began as a three-acre play area with computer labs intended to carry the children's television program's educational initiatives into communities later expanded to 14 acres of rollercoasters, rides for kids of most ages, and a considerable waterpark – and it remains one of two *Sesame Street* parks nationwide. While its Mexican counterpart *Parque Plaza Sesamo* draws more than a million visitors annually, the Philly original continues to find success with expansions and a newly-announced year-round schedule that began in January 2021.

Despite more than two dozen rides and a host of food and souvenir shops, the main attraction for most children remains the cast of roughly 20 Muppets roaming the park and performing at stage shows and parades regularly.

A variety of interactive performances featuring Muppet characters (and often a human cast member or two) fill the day at small theaters around the park, and a spectacular song and dance parade steals the show twice daily - check the schedule and designate someone in your group to stake out a spot along the parade route an hour early if you want the front row experience. Special holiday shows draw big crowds at Halloween and Christmas, and regular firework displays light up the night in warmer months.

In its continuing effort to improve the world for children, Sesame Place has nabbed a couple of other notable firsts over the years. In 2007, it became the first theme park in the state to go completely smoke-free, and in 2018 it became the world's first theme park to be accredited as a Certified Autism Center by the International Board of Credentialing and Continuing Education Standards, certifying staff and the property for a range of specific needs for guests on the autism spectrum.

Address 100 Sesame Road, Langhorne PA 19047, +1 (215) 702-3566, www.sesameplace.com |
Getting there By car, take I-95 N to Exit 5A onto US-1 N and exit at N Oxford Valley
Road. Follow the signs to destination. | Hours See website for seasonal hours and events |
Tip More family fun is just 10 minutes away at Shady Brook Farm, with year-round events,
you-pick fields, tours, and a deli (931 Stony Hill Road, Yardley, www.shadybrookfarm.com).

86_Shrek Box

Leave an ogre, take an ogre

Philadelphia's favorite monster is undoubtedly the orange enigma that is Gritty (it wouldn't be fair to call the Phillie Phanatic a monster, as he's officially a bird – so we can leave that potential rivalry alone). But the residents of South Philly appear to have a strong affinity for another green monster unrelated to local sports. A little green box known as the Shrek Box became a neighborhood staple so faithfully visited by its followers that it was officially categorized as a "religious destination" on Google Maps.

If you're a superfan of Shrek, you may just have a religious experience here; otherwise, it's still certainly worth a visit for that only-in-Philadelphia chuckle you get when you pull open the door and peek inside. Well, not *only* in Philadelphia anymore – at least one known copycat has popped up in Denver!

When the print news industry scaled back daily deliveries but left their newspaper boxes behind, strewn about the city streets with no purpose, Wil Keiper and Lauren Devlin felt the natural evolution of a neighborhood box was to make it a repository for all things ogre, specifically Shrek. They painted the box in Shrek's instantly recognizable skin tone (a swampy yet vibrant green), added a few familiar phrases and icons to the exterior, and filled the interior with copies of the film and other memorabilia. The box encouraged the public, "Leave a Shrek, Take a Shrek."

It may have seemed like a hair-brained scheme initially, but locals love it, with Keiper reporting multiple daily visits. The contents now branch out from exclusively Shrek merch to include fan art and notes, video games, and even crafts, like an embroidered onion (because "ogres are like onions," according to one of the film's most famous scenes). The Shrek Box is even decorated for holidays, but it's a true sight to behold any time of year, now just a few blocks north of its original address.

Address 8th & Catharine Streets, Philadelphia, PA 19147, www.instagram.com/shrek.box |
Getting there Bus 47, 47M to 8th Street & Catharine Street | Hours Unrestricted | Tip
If you leave here with a hankering for quality onions, the Sunday Headhouse Farmers
Market is one of the city's largest and is under a mile away (2nd Street & Lombard Street,
www.thefoodtrust.org).

87 — Sidewalk Pretzel

A beloved symbol of the city

As both a shape and a food, there's no symbol that could truly represent Philadelphia better than the pretzel. From the symbolic central knot demonstrating the strength found when our community weaves together in just the right way, as it's done countless times since the founding of the nation, to the mouth-watering deliciousness that derives from a humble strip of dough prepared – and salted – just so, the pretzel *is* Philadelphia.

Gone are the days when soft pretzels were hawked on filthy street corners by questionable vendors, who were often equally as filthy, shoving stacks of doughy delight through car windows with bare hands, though it wasn't long ago that this was commonplace. Today, you have to pop into a soft pretzel shop to purchase these quintessentially Philadelphian treats properly, but you'll have no difficulty finding one – they're everywhere, as well they should be. And there's one corner in Philadelphia where you can still find a pretzel whenever the urge strikes you. You just can't eat it.

At the intersection of Schell and Pemberton Streets in Bella Vista, look for the bright blue door, and then look down at the square of sidewalk directly in front of it, where you'll find a perfect, shiny pretzel gleaming back at you.

This picturesque token was embedded here by homeowners Randi and Mike Lawson when some nasty sewer troubles forced them to repave their sidewalk. Rather than simply grumble their way through the unexpected expense, they turned a trash situation into pure treasure in true Philly style. For them, the pretzel isn't just a representation of the city they love. It also pays homage to their former family cat, Pretzel, who was particularly fond of contorting her hairless body into knots of her own. And, in case you're curious about the origins of this perfect little piece of sidewalk art, it was once a novelty bottle opener.

Address Schell & Pemberton Streets, Philadelphia, PA 19147 | Getting there Bus 47, 47M to 8th & Fitzwater Streets | Hours Unrestricted from the outside only | Tip Around the corner, Pemberton Street is a tiny alley filled with the shimmering mosaic art of Isaiah Zagar (Pemberton Street, www.instagram.com/isaiahzagar).

88_ Singh Center

An architectural jewel

Philadelphia is not often ranked among America's top cities for architecture, but a handful of its modern buildings are clear head-turners, and the Krishna P. Singh Center for Nanotechnology on the University of Pennsylvania campus is a masterpiece among them. If you've seen it, you may have thought you were on the set of a futuristic film (and the university has turned down plenty of requests for filming here), but this building is the research home of both the School of Arts and Sciences and the School of Engineering and Applied Sciences.

Within its 78,000 square feet are state-of-the-art labs and equipment unfound in other major cities. Engineering of the basement had to account for housing sensitive microscopes that range in structural requirements from eliminating all electromagnetic field interference to guaranteeing no vibration – a difficult feat in a busy city and an active building, where even elevators produce vibrations.

You won't be able to access the underground equipment, but you'll certainly notice the ground floor's clean-room fabrication lab with its orange glass walls (needed to block ambient UV light) and the orange accents it inspired around the building. Other than the green lawn of its quad, orange is just about the only color you'll find on this shiny exterior of metal and glass, and do take note of all that glass allowing you to engage with the important research happening within.

Impossible to miss, the floating cantilever hovering above the quad is a 68-foot-long forum that serves as a lecture hall and conference space and has helped the building win numerous architecture and design awards. You're welcome to rest on the lawn below and enjoy the courtyard on a sunny afternoon, but you'll also want to catch sight of this building at night, when the orange glow from within emanates through its all-glass front, a signal of the future dawning here.

Address 3205 Walnut Street, Philadelphia, PA 19104, www.nano.upenn.edu, info@nano.upenn.edu | Getting there Bus 30, 42, 49, LUCYGR to 33rd & Walnut Streets | Hours Viewable from the outside only | Tip Headquartered in Philly, the Science History Institute has a free museum with both permanent and temporary exhibits (315 Chestnut Street, www.sciencehistory.org/museum).

89__Sister Cities Park

Where Philly is the center of everything

Hometown pride is a fairly universal concept, but few citizens are quite as protective of their place and unabashedly proud of their reputation as Philadelphians. So much so that you may even wonder if some here think the city sits in the center of the world map. It doesn't, of course, but there's one spot where everything does appear to revolve around Philadelphia, and that's in Sister Cities Park. It's a bit ironic that this public space was designed to honor *other* cities, Philadelphia's international counterparts, but there's something apropos about this particular Philly flex.

Among the many highlights of Sister Cities Park is the interactive World Fountain in the southern half of its Logan location. Here, carved in bluestone, is a unique representation of the world with Philadelphia at its core. The abstract globe otherwise displays only Philly's sister cities, identified by name and distance from Philadelphia, of course, engraved in the component pavers supporting the water feature. The water itself is the most intriguing element of the fountain and, perhaps the whole park, not just because it's fun to stomp around in, but because it launches skyward from eleven jets (one for each sister city), with streams proportional to their respective cities' distances.

Philadelphia gained its 11th sister city in 2017 with Frankfurt am Main, Germany joining the family that began with Florence, Italy, and Tel Aviv, Israel, and has grown to include cities in Japan, Cameroon, Poland, Korea, and beyond. Sister Cities International pairs US cities with diverse locations around the world seeking to strengthen cultural and economic bonds through citizen diplomacy. The concept has existed since 1956, when it was proposed by the Eisenhower administration. Use it as an excuse to add some new places to your bucket list, or just bring the kids to splash in the water jets.

Address 210 N 18th Street, Philadelphia, PA 19103, +1 (215) 440-5500, www.centercityphila.org, info@centercityphila.org | Getting there Bus 32 to 18th & Vine Streets | Hours Daily 6–1am | Tip Beyond the fountain, at the far southern tip of the park, *AMOR*, the sculpture by Robert Indiana that graced the Museum of Art's steps for the arrival of Pope Francis, has found its forever home (1300 Locust Street, www.hsp.org).

90 _ Skew Arch Bridge

Better below than above

No one is quite sure when this bridge was built, and it served little purpose for decades. But Philadelphia Streets Department's Bridge #704 is the most mesmerizing relic of an abandoned era of Philly transit history remaining in the city today.

There are better names for this bridge than its mere numerical designation. Many call it the Skew Arch Bridge, referencing the 15 brick arches supporting the stone structure, and it's these arches that dazzled in-the-know photographers and the lucky few who've stumbled across them while traversing West Fairmount Park over the years.

The intricate brickwork pattern suggests the bridge was built in the late 1800s, aligning with the knowledge that it once served the Fairmount Park Trolley, which was launched in 1896 and closed in 1946. It wasn't only trolley service that rapidly disappeared just after World War II, when Fairmount Park Transit Company vanished, though. Through comprehensive sales of all equipment, virtually nothing remains today of this piece of Philly history other than the remarkable little bridge still standing today and scattered pieces of rail infrastructure throughout the park. In fact, so little remains now that the discovery of an ornate power pole cap during a 2017 project to revamp the area for hikers and bikers was celebrated as a precious find.

Until recently, the bridge remained known primarily to two small groups: mountain bikers, whose jaunts re-wore rough paths around the bridge, and a tiny number of hostel guests trekking the woodsy, awkward trail to Chamounix Mansion, a reminder of the structure's other popular nickname, Chamounix Drive Bridge. Today, the bridge has been stabilized as part of the Trolley Trail Project, welcoming Philadelphians back to this section of previously overlooked park with clear trails for hiking, biking, and even horseback riding.

Address Conshohocken Avenue & Falls Road, Philadelphia, PA 19131, +1 (215) 988-9334, www.myphillypark.org | Getting there Bus 38 to Conshohocken Avenue & E Country Club Road | Hours Daily dawn–dusk | Tip At the opposite end of the trail, Chamounix Mansion is an 1802 house that was nearly demolished until a hostel saved it. Today it's on the NRHP (3250 Chamounix Drive, www.hiusa.org).

91 Southeast Asian Market

An enormous market you've somehow missed

You can stop searching for the most authentic Thai food in Philadelphia, and the same goes for Laotian, Cambodian, and more. Since roughly 1985 (no one quite remembers the exact date), the Southeast Asian Market in FDR Park has been selling the most tantalizing Southeast Asian bites prepared by the community and, largely, for the community. Even today, about 70% of the customers identify as Southeast Asian (SEA) themselves, though everyone is encouraged to dive into this pop-up culinary kingdom.

The market now shifts between two locations seasonally. The spring market is held near the park's Broad Street entrance from April to late June, and the summer session runs into November next to Taney Field. Depending on the day, you'll find between 40–70 vendors dishing out plates you might expect, like coconut rice, papaya salad, pho, and barbecue meats, but you're almost guaranteed to uncover something new, no matter how well-traveled you are. Look for gems like the Malaysian *murtabak* crepe stuffed with curried meat and potatoes; Indonesian lamb skewers with peanut sauce and rice cakes; and Vietnamese *bánh xèo*, a pork-stuffed turmeric rice pancake. Wash it down with real Vietnamese iced coffee or the Thai version, *oliang*. There are plenty of sweet drinks filled with delicious add-ins, like basil seeds and grass jelly too.

If you're looking to elevate your pantry, there are vendors selling harder-to-find ingredients that will make your home-cooked endeavors considerably more authentic, too. Look for bounty like Thai eggplant, fish mint, kaffir lime, jackfruit, and the ever divisive and fragrant durian at the market.

This whole enterprise is believed to have begun with a single Lao woman selling papaya salad and barbecued chicken wings on a stick. Today it is a thriving community of regulars celebrating and sharing their heritage with all who pass through.

Address See website for seasonal locations, 1500 Pattison Avenue & South Broad Street, Philadelphia, PA 19145, www.fdrseamarket.com, info@fdrseamarket.com | Getting there Subway to NRG Station (Broad Street Line); Bus 17, 68 to Broad Street & Zinkoff Boulevard–MBNS | Hours Seasonally, Sat & Sun 10am–6pm | Tip In need of harder-to-find ingredients while the market is closed for the season? Chai Hong Market is one of many SEA specialty shops along 7th Street on either side of W Moyamensing Avenue (2200 S 7th Street).

92 St. Albans Place

From Devil's Pocket to romantic courtyard

The 2300 block of St. Albans Place has been closed to vehicular traffic since the days of the horse and buggy. Formed in 1870 to house the influx of new industrial workers filling the neighborhood, the space between these two rows of townhomes was left as a communal garden running the entire length of the block when the structures were first built. While this surprising feature has always been appreciated by residents throughout its more than 150 years, it has not always been the picture of romance it is today.

It wasn't long after its creation that the working-class neighborhood developed an unseemly reputation for petty crime and even some danger. According to local legend, it earned the nickname, "The Devil's Pocket," when a priest claimed that the lawless children of this area were so fearless they would "steal the watch from the devil's pocket." This is certainly not the vibe today, though part of the area maintains the old nickname out of tradition.

Instead, the Graduate Hospital neighborhood, as it's now known, is far from undesirable, and the Second Empire-style homes of St. Albans find themselves surrounding an immaculately kept garden of mature plantings mirrored by the equally impressive window boxes flanking the space.

The red brick courtyard offers a terribly romantic stroll around the elongated garden, particularly in late summer, when the tableau is at its most lush, evoking the society garden strolls of yore (though they certainly never happened here). When you come to take your own lazy turn about the garden, keep an eye peeled for house number 2302 (it's on the southeast corner of the courtyard). The door has been replaced, but this was the home of young Cole Sear in *The Sixth Sense*, the highest grossing horror film of all time until 2017. Bruce Willis' character, Malcolm Crowe, sat on the bench across the courtyard, waiting for him.

Address St. Albans Place, Philadelphia, PA 19146 | **Getting there** Bus 12 to Grays Ferry Avenue & Fitzwater Street | **Hours** Unrestricted | **Tip** Continue your *Sixth Sense* journey with a visit to St. Augustine Church, where Cole takes refuge and chats with [spoiler] already-dead Malcolm (243 N Lawrence Street, www.st-augustinechurch.com).

93 St. John Neumann's Body

A holy body permanently on display

Whether you're among the Catholic faithful or simply curious to gaze upon the actual body of America's first male saint, the National Shrine of St. John Neumann makes St. Peter the Apostle Church a worthwhile visit for most. Here, on full display in a glass tomb, the body of long-deceased St. John Neumann (1811–1860), patron saint of sick children and immigrants, lies clad in Roman vestments, receiving visitors regularly. And you're welcome to be among them.

Though he passed more than a century and a half ago and was originally buried more traditionally in this same church at the time, reports of miraculous health recoveries attributed to the Philadelphia bishop long after his death reached the Vatican and ultimately resulted in Pope John Paul II canonizing him as the first male saint from the United States in 1977. Prior to this, in 1962, the soon-to-be-saint's body was exhumed and discovered to be in reportedly great condition, but a sculpted mask has covered his face since he returned to the public gaze.

Curiously, the saint's wardrobe has changed a couple of times through the subsequent decades and, even more curiously, neither his body nor his mask suffered any damage when the entire pulpit next to him was eviscerated in a potentially devastating fire in 2009, adding yet another potential miracle to St. John Neumann's record.

While the saint himself is the main draw, there's an equally intriguing "museum" here too in the form of a small collection of brow-raising objects connected to St. John Neumann's Philadelphia life. Preserved now in a clear tomb of its own, the saint's original coffin is on prominent display, as are the step on which he collapsed before dying and, most curious of all, the noose used to hang two criminal brothers who were successfully convinced to repent by the then-bishop just before their dramatic demises.

Address 1019 N 5th Street, Philadelphia, PA 19123, +1 (215) 627-3080, www.stjohnneumann.org, sjnoffice@comcast.net | Getting there Light Rail to Girard Avenue & 5th Street (15 Line) | Hours Mon–Sat 10am–6:30pm, Sun 7am–4:30pm | Tip The Cathedral Basilica of Saints Peter and Paul is the largest church in the state, and Pope Francis celebrated mass here in 2015 during the World Meeting of Families (1723 Race Street, www.cathedralphila.org).

94__ Star Doors
Philly's most coveted glass

Roughly 100 years after their original production in Philadelphia, handcrafted "star doors" of elegantly etched glass and handsomely carved wood are rising to, well, *stardom* once again. But supply is limited.

Stroll the streets of historic neighborhoods, and you're likely to spot at least one of these glass-paned front doors, each emblazoned with a central starburst encased by one of several wooden designs. The doors were designed and produced by Arthur Tofani Lumber & Millwork on South 8th Street perhaps as early as the 1920s, using glass produced by H. Perilstein Glass Company. There was no exclusive deal here, and plenty of rival millworkers were able to mimic the theme, accounting for the variation in both shape and quality still found around the city today. The ease of knocking off the design may have been an irritation to Tofani and its customers a century ago, but it proves a blessing for treasure hunters today, allowing more doors to escape the perils of passing time.

While star doors may have originally hung in more isolated neighborhoods, you'll find them scattered farther about town now. They're not being reproduced anymore, but savvy shoppers looking to include some historic authenticity to their modern remodels are snapping them up as soon as they become available. Chris Stock, owner of Philadelphia Salvage, says his employees have become the de facto historic door experts in the city, and star doors have never been more popular. "You can't get the glass anymore, but we can rebuild the doors," he says. "Someone once found half of one on the side of the street. It's on her house now," he adds, demonstrating just how desperate Philly homeowners are to snag one of these subtle pieces of local design history. Finding one on the curb is a near miracle, but star-spotting on hinges around the city makes for a fun scavenger hunt on any lazy afternoon.

Address 817 Livingston Street, Philadelphia, PA 19125 | Getting there Bus 89 to Norris & Belgrade Streets | Hours Viewable from the outside only | Tip In addition to custom restoration, Philadelphia Salvage has a retail space worth exploring. You might just find a star door, but call them "Hollywood doors" here when inquiring (2234 W Westmoreland Street, www.philadelphiasalvage.com).

95 Surgical Amphitheater

You've seen them on TV, now see one in person

Pennsylvania Hospital is full of firsts. Perhaps most importantly, its 1751 founding makes it the first true hospital in the United States. (New York City's Bellevue Hospital makes a claim for this title, having opened six beds in an almshouse in 1736, but that is a story for another conversation.)

The historic hospital is also home to the country's first medical library, opened in 1762. But the most fascinating first here is its surgical amphitheater.

You've seen just this type of room in period films: cavernous, circular spaces with an operating table in the center and a crowd of curious onlookers. Generally featured is a screaming patient in utter agony. Unfortunately, these Hollywood plots are not exaggerations, as this is exactly the scene that played out in this very room for decades. At least for the poor.

Keep in mind this was the 18th century, so there was no electricity, anesthesia, or real understanding of hygiene or sanitation. For those of little means, a trip to the surgical amphitheater was charity. The doctors here were among some of the country's most revered, but the ambiance was abysmal. Doctors relied on sunlight for visibility, tools were rudimentary at best, and patients were given a choice of alcohol, laudanum, or a mallet to the head (honestly) to distract them from the pain.

The result? Most patients could be heard screaming them from outside the hospital walls as doctors worked as quickly as possible on their fully-conscious bodies.

Surgical theaters are occasionally still in use for educational purposes, though now you'll find the sterile, white environments of modern hospitals, and patients are mercifully anesthetized. You can tour the original here by reservation, and thank your lucky stars that medicine has evolved.

Address 800 Spruce Street, Philadelphia, PA 19107, +1 (215) 829-5434, www.pennmedicine.org | Getting there Bus 12, 47, 47M to 8th & Pine Streets | Hours By reservation only | Tip Pennsylvania Hospital was the brainchild of Dr. Thomas Bond, whose 1769 house is now a bed and breakfast in Old City (129 S 2nd Street, www.thomasbondhousebandb.com).

96__ Taller Puertorriqueño
The cultural heart of El Barrio

North Philadelphia's Fairhill neighborhood is home to the city's greatest concentration of Puerto Rican residents, and this is where you'll find *el centro de oro*, "the golden block." Throughout the arts-rich neighborhood, you'll encounter enough music, dancing, murals, and restaurants to keep you immersed in Latinx culture all day, even without a set itinerary. And make it a point to visit Taller Puertorriqueño while you're here.

Originally established as a small cultural community in 1974, Taller Puertorriqueño is now the most prominent Latin arts organization in the entire state. In 2016, the non-profit moved to its current 24,000-square-foot space, containing dance studios, performance space, gardens, a bilingual bookstore, and a gallery. President Nasheli Juliana Ortiz González says Taller is known as the cultural heart of the neighborhood not just because of the extensive programming and outreach it offers, but also because it's a neutral space. "It's the point to meet and celebrate our similarities and discuss our differences," she says, adding that Taller is unique among arts organizations in its heavy focus on social justice work achieved through cultural exploration.

Though larger in its current home, the Lorenzo Homar Gallery is still the region's only gallery devoted to Puerto Rican and Latinx art. When you visit, you'll experience the current exhibit and also a permanent collection of works donated by artists from previous exhibits, adding to the cumulative cultural education offered by Taller.

Exhibits here aren't selected solely by art advisors and curators, either. In keeping with its commitment to the neighborhood it serves, Taller's community members weigh in on each selection, too. To immerse yourself even more in the culture and the area, make a reservation on Taller's website for a neighborhood tour, largely focused on local murals.

Address 2600 N 5th Street, Philadelphia, PA 19133, +1 (215) 426-3311, www.tallerpr.org | Getting there Bus 39, 47 to 5th & Huntingdon Streets | Hours Mon 9am–5pm, Tue–Sat 10am–6pm | Tip The neighborhood's legendary, hands-on music store, Centro Musical, is just up the street. Look for the trio of metal palm trees out front (464 W Lehigh Avenue, www.facebook.com/centromusicalpa).

97 __ Tea for Few at Stenton

The hot drink wasn't for everyone in early Philly

The British may be inexorably linked to tea in today's public consciousness, but that wasn't always the case. At the time of William Penn's arrival in what would become Philadelphia, England had only recently begun to experience China's teas, and it certainly wasn't widely available. By the time Penn's secretary built his country house, Stenton, 50 years later in 1730, tea had made its way to England's upper classes. But it was still difficult to acquire in the American colonies, even for the rich. This secretary was James Logan, whose family name survives all over the city today, and Stenton is now a remarkably-preserved historic house open to visitors since 1900. Inside is a tea service collection, and few realize its significance.

Merely drinking tea in 1730s Philadelphia was a sign of status. Owning a full set of fine porcelain tea service indicated one was not just wealthy, but also influential. Who else would be hosting visitors important enough to share tea with? This remained true even through the end of the 18th century, when tea became more readily available to colonial masses – more could drink it, but few owned the finery for serving it.

James Logan had been personally importing tea to Philadelphia as early as 1713, and excavations around Stenton reveal the house was home to an astonishing assortment of tea equipage, much of it originally dating to the mid-1700s. Take a look at some of the collection in Stenton's parlor, and consider those who passed through for tea. Franklin, Washington, and Jefferson each visited Stenton several times, and this was briefly the headquarters of General Howe. Marvel at the rest of the house too. Unlike most historic homes, this one has been untouched since the mid-19th century, when it ceased serving as the family home. Not even electricity or plumbing altered Stenton, let alone renovation.

Address 4601 N 18th Street, Philadelphia, PA 19140, +1 (215) 329-7312, www.stenton.org, information@stenton.org | Getting there Bus 75 to Courtland & 18th Streets | Hours Apr–Dec, Tue–Sat 1–4pm; Jan–Mar by appointment only | Tip Logan also owned silver service from 1723 or 1724, now in the collection of the Philadelphia Museum of Art (2600 Benjamin Franklin Parkway, www.philamuseum.org).

98 Thaddeus Kosciuszko National Memorial

Smallest national park site, big dose of history

Of more than 420 national park sites across the United States, Philadelphia holds the honor of being home to the very smallest one, the Thaddeus Kosciuszko National Memorial. If you were picturing vast swaths like Grand Canyon National Park, understand that the majority of sites administered by the National Park Service aren't nearly that large, and they aren't even what you'd consider parks at all. Like this one.

This 0.02-acre plot was once the home of Polish-born Revolutionary War hero Thaddeus Kosciuszko. An engineer who floated between forts during the war, Kosciuszko never had a known home on this side of the Atlantic until he returned *after* the war and demanded the pay he was owed by the new United States Congress. It's then that he rented a room in Philadelphia, having asked his secretary to find something small, cheap, and remote. Small and cheap he may have gotten, but it's just around the corner from Independence Hall, so "remote" was a bit of a miss. He didn't spend much time here, so, fittingly, but you'll find some period furnishings and a short film, alongside some explanation of Kosciuszko's military engineering accomplishments.

Though he was not nearly as successful in his home country, he's certainly better known in Poland than he is here, despite the magnitude of American parks, structures, and even towns named for him. Perhaps his most intriguing claim to fame for a modern audience was his close connection to Thomas Jefferson, who visited him at his room here and helped him draft his will. In that will, Kosciuszko decreed that his estate be used to free as many slaves as possible.

This tiniest of park sites is only open seasonally, and usually on weekends, but it's certainly worth checking off your NPS bucket list.

Address 301 Pine Street, Philadelphia, PA 19106, +1 (215) 965-2305, www.nps.gov |
Getting there Bus 12, 40 to Pine & 3rd Streets | Hours Apr–Oct, Sat & Sun noon–4pm |
Tip The Polish American Cultural Center is home to a small, free museum devoted to Polish
heritage in Philadelphia and beyond (308 Walnut Street, www.polishamericancenter.org).

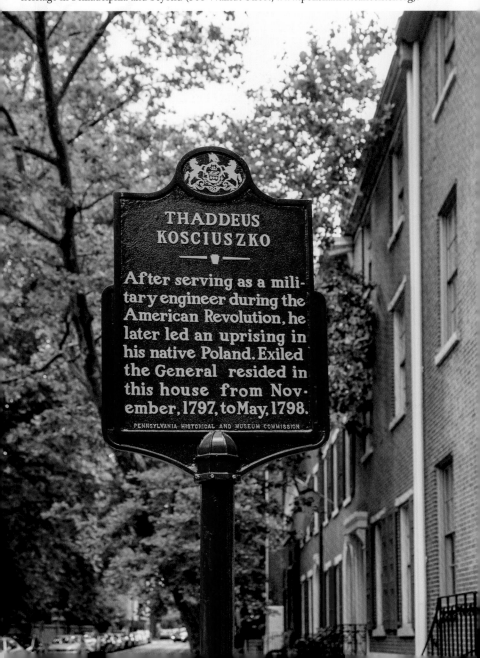

99 _ Thirsty Dice

Eat, drink, play, and propose?

You might think a gaming café couldn't be Philadelphia's most romantic destination, and you'd probably be right about that. Yet Thirsty Dice *is* the scene of many a Philly first date, and some of the initial connections forged here have blossomed into marriages. In fact, on the same day that the space witnessed a proposal in early 2022, another couple came by to take engagement photos because they, too, also met in this little zone of Philly fun.

If you're happily taken or simply not interested in looking for love right now, don't fret – this isn't a meat market. Thirsty Dice is a gaming café with more than 800 games in its playable library, and about 200 for sale, alongside gaming parts (like dice, of course) and merch. Primarily, this is a spot for sitting down for some fun with friends and favorite games, or even ones you've never heard of – the staff, or Gametenders, here are fluent in all things game and can make recommendations for new adventures. Best of all, they'll tell you how to play the game, so you don't waste the day reading complicated rules.

To keep you fueled throughout your play, you'll also find a few menus here: food, drinks, and a dedicated ice cream menu. Top recommendations include the short rib cheesesteak on a seeded roll and the bananas foster boozy milkshake (there are half a dozen flavors of these adult delights, so banana-haters have options, too). Traditional ice creams are scooped from Philly favorite Bassetts and local Herman's Coffee developed a "Roll with It" blend exclusively for Thirsty Dice. If beer is your beverage of choice, you'll be most excited to find more than a dozen brews on tap (wine and cocktails, too). You may not be in the mood for games, so rest assured that you're welcome to come by just for bites or sips. But at least consider snagging some new dice from the "gumball" machine on your way out.

Address N 17th Street & Fairmount Avenue, Philadelphia, PA 19130, +1 (215) 765-2679, www.thirstydice.com | Getting there Bus 2 to 17th & North Streets; Subway to Fairmount (Broad Street Line) | Hours Tue–Thu 3–10pm, Fri 3pm–midnight, Sat 10am–midnight, Sun 10am–7pm | Tip Herman's Coffee & Market is so much more than just a coffee shop (1313 S 3rd Street, www.hermanscoffee.com).

100_ Thunderbird Salvage

Bargaining for local treasures

Snooping isn't polite, but let's face it: we love it. While it's frowned upon to go treasure hunting in people's private closets and attics, you can easily get your fix at quality thrift shops, especially ones like the cavernous Thunderbird Salvage, where a good chunk of the inventory comes from local clean-outs and storage units. Get an up-close look at the coolest, quirkiest, and most bizarre items formerly hidden inside Philadelphia homes. And you can take them to your home.

Owner George Mathes launched Thunderbird Salvage in 2010 as an online business operating out of a warehouse. You can still browse inventory and even purchase through Instagram DMs and a quick Venmo payment, but you can now browse in person, too, and it's an experience you don't want to miss. When the First Church of Our Lord Jesus Christ in Fishtown was listed for sale, Mathes snapped it up in 2015, hoping to forestall gentrification by keeping ownership of local buildings local. Today, it's filled with the antiques, vintage, and general oddities of Thunderbird Salvage.

Exploring the sanctuary of goodies here, you'll certainly find plenty of local nostalgia, and you may even stumble into the deeply intimate, like the personal diary of an area teenager penned in the 1980s. Whether you're looking for a fabulous antique sofa, auto-graphed posters, or some socially acceptable snooping, it's all here.

For locals who love the business, it's not just the reasonable prices that draw their attention to Thunderbird Salvage. There's a social mis-sion to thrifting that keeps materials out of landfills, puts less demand on new manufacturing, reduces the carbon footprint of transporting merchandise, and, on a more personal level, keeps Philly's treasures in Philly. Still, there *is* something about snagging a deal that adds some appeal. At Thunderbird Salvage, you can respectfully haggle flea-market-style.

Address 2441 Frankford Avenue, Philadelphia, PA 19125, +1 (267) 761-4336, www.instagram.com/thunderbirdsalvage | *Getting there* Bus 5 to Frankford Avenue & Cumberland Street | *Hours* Daily 9am–7pm | *Tip* You can scope out vintage variety (and more) at Jinxed Fishtown, down the street. There are a few locations of this local chain now, but each is curated for its neighborhood (1331 Frankford Street, www.instagram.com/jinxedstore).

101 Tomb of Empress Ana María

Final resting place of Mexico's first empress

For a city founded on democratic principles, it's not surprising that signs of monarchy are few in Philadelphia – but they're not entirely absent. Tucked away in the nondescript graveyard of St. John the Evangelist Roman Catholic Church is the tomb of Ana María Josefa Ramona de Huarte y Muñiz, First Empress of Mexico.

A Spanish noblewoman by birth, she married Agustín de Iturbide, who would later become president and then emperor of Mexico in 1822. But in a story all too familiar to early Philadelphians, revolution came shortly after. All told, Ana María's head was crowned for less than a year before she and her ostentatious husband were exiled to Europe for a period nearly as brief. In 1824, they returned to Mexico unaware that a trap had been laid, and her husband was swiftly executed. Fortunately for the former empress, she and her children were permitted to flee and were even given an annual pension from the Mexican government, though they would never live in royal style again.

The ex-royals bounced around between several US cities before settling on Philadelphia, where they eventually slipped away into relative obscurity before Empress Ana María died in 1861, virtually unknown to Philadelphia society, as she remains to this day.

It's quite easy to have an audience with the empress today. St. John the Evangelist is a very active church, but you don't need to worry about interrupting mass schedules to get to the graveyard. The empress is buried in vault IX, bordering the public sidewalk on Ludlow Street, on the north side of the church, with only an unobtrusive fence between. Garnering even less recognition of their illustrious ancestry, three of Ana María's children and one of her grandchildren are also buried in this vault. But the discreet inscription reads only, "Vault of A. M. H. de YTURBIDE."

Address 21 S 13th Street, Philadelphia, PA 19107, +1 (215) 563-4145, www.stjohnsphilly.org | Getting there Subway to 13th Street (Market–Frankford Line); Light Rail to 13th Street (Lines 10, 11, 13, 34, 36) | Hours Unrestricted | Tip For another glimpse of royal history, head to the East Falls neighborhood, where you'll find the childhood home of Grace Kelly, who became Princess of Monaco when Prince Rainier III married her in 1965 (3901 Henry Avenue).

102_ Urban Fishing

Country fun in the city

Quick: Imagine someone fishing! Did you picture someone in a bucket hat standing by the shore of a reedy lake? Or perhaps someone reeling in a thrashing swordfish on the ocean? It's okay, most of us saw a version of one of these, but you don't need to head to the country or hit the high seas to fish safely in the Philadelphia area. You can cast a line just off Columbus Boulevard in Pennsport, and it's legal.

At the end of the Delaware River Trail, the Delaware River Waterfront Corporation unveiled Pier 68 in 2015 with the express objective of encouraging catch-and-release fishing from this scenic spot on the river. You'll need to be properly licensed by the State in order to fish here, and you're expected to return your haul to the waters below after reeling it in, but there's no other *catch* here. Show up, head to the end of the pier, and try your luck. You may snag anything from bass and trout to shad and sturgeon. And don't be surprised if you hear, "Any luck today?" more than once. It's not too common to spot people fishing around Philadelphia, and curious onlookers are keen to strike up a chat here when they do.

If you'd rather just watch the action, there are plenty of undulating benches here to rest upon—they mimic the tide below and are surprisingly comfortable for a public lie-down, though it's also fine to simply sit. To make a day of it, pack a basket and head to the pier's Picnic Grove when you're hungry. Here you'll find plenty of seating among trees and landscaping you may be surprised to find perched upon a river. In the meantime, sunbathe on the lawn, read a book in the shade, or take a stroll along the water-side walking trail as the anglers cast their lines above. All you have to do to spend a glorious day in the great outdoors is pass through the native trees at the pier's entrance, strategically placed to block the city sights behind.

Address 1751 South Columbus Boulevard, Philadelphia, PA 19148, +1 (215) 922-2386, www.delawareriverwaterfront.com, info@drwc.org | Getting there Bus 7, 25, 29, 64 to Pier 70 Walmart & Home Depot | Hours Daily dawn–dusk | Tip From here, you can also walk north along the Delaware River Trail, which saw rapid expansion in Spring 2022 (Pier 68, www.delawareriverwaterfront.com).

103_ W Hotel WET Deck Bar

Have a drink with a couple of legends

Atop the seventh floor of W Hotel Philadelphia is a swanky green space tucked beyond a vibrant, modern bar scene. Here among the hedges, you may encounter a couple of historical figures who will remind you that you're still in Philly. Well, at least one of them will.

Most of this W Hotel is heavily influenced by Philadelphia heritage, both historical and cultural, and it's well worth your time to stroll around its public spaces from the lobby to the secret saloon (especially necessary for Grace Kelly fans). Then head to WET Deck Bar, grab a drink, and take it to the Secret Garden for a surprising escape in the heart of Center City.

You can easily find your own personal space to sip with friends and snack on bites from the bar menu amidst the topiaries and myrtle trees. And make sure to say hello to the illuminated busts of Ben Franklin and Marie Antoinette, his acquaintance during his time serving as the country's first foreign ambassador. With this in mind, take note of the many other European influences around this contemporary take on the formal French garden, which was the model for many early Philadelphia gardens and even for the landscape design of some of our parks.

Use of the pool at WET Deck is generally reserved for hotel guests, though you can gain access by reserving a cabana or booking a spa treatment. But take a stroll around and notice how it adds to the funkified formal garden vibes of the cohesive space, from leaf-green seating in the shape of hedgerows to large topiaries shielding concrete views beyond. And ogle the mosaic work of not just the pool's parterre patterns, but also of the bar's showstopping, floor-to-ceiling floral pieces.

You won't completely forget you're in Philadelphia while you're here – you're certainly not supposed to! But if you begin to lose your orientation, you can always hang on to the unparalleled view of City Hall.

Address 1439 Chestnut Street, Philadelphia, PA 19102, +1 (215) 709-8000, www.marriott.com | Getting there Bus 9, 21, 38, 42, 124, 125 to Chestnut & Broad Streets | Hours Fri–Sun 11am–7pm | Tip Interested in trying your own hand at mosaic art after viewing WET Deck's spectacles? Try a class at Bella Mosaic Art (6780 Germantown Avenue, www.bellamosaic.com).

104_Wagner Free Institute

Free science lessons in a Victorian museum

Philadelphia is full of blasts from its colonial past, with original 18th-century exteriors and restored interiors throughout Old City and beyond. While there are far fewer examples of Victorian heritage sharing Philly's historical spotlight, the Wagner Free Institute of Science proves that the city's best-preserved glimpse of the past may actually come from the 19th century. Head to North Central Philadelphia to explore the 1855 science museum with interior exhibits as original as the classical revival exterior, and you'll achieve a nearly identical experience to that of the countless students and gawkers who've walked the wooden floors before you.

The Wagner Free Institute was founded as a free science education center for adults and continues to offer college-level lectures at no charge today. Drop in for lessons on botany, paleontology, plagues, and more, delivered by esteemed professors from Philadelphia's top universities and visiting scientists of national renown. While the Wagner has succeeded in altering as little as possible since its inception, one very welcome change expanded the institute's mission from educating adults only to educating people of all ages, and there are now plenty of children's programs both onsite and as a traveling service.

While the complimentary classes are a local goldmine of opportunities to expand your horizons, you'll still love the institute even if you have no desire to dredge up memories of student life. Upstairs, the second floor houses a natural sciences museum of more than 100,000 specimens, from minerals to taxidermy animals, including the first saber-toothed tiger found in North America. But what's most intriguing about the collection is its unchanged arrangement, granting rare insight into the academic mindset of the Victorian era. Don't miss the original, handwritten labels of the insect displays.

Address 1700 W Montgomery Avenue, Philadelphia, PA 19121, +1 (215) 763-6529, www.wagnerfreeinstitute.org, info@wagnerfreeinstitute.org | Getting there Bus 3 to Cecil B Moore Avenue & 17th Street | Hours Tue–Fri 9:30am–4:30pm, see website for tours and class schedule | Tip Head 10 minutes north for the quirky Historical Dental Museum at the Temple University School of Dentistry, where the highlight is the bucket of teeth (322 N Broad Street, www.temple.pastperfectonline.com).

105__West Laurel Hill

Where America's best came to rest

Though they're sister cemeteries, it's important to keep in mind that Laurel Hill Cemetery and West Laurel Hill Cemetery are not the same collection of final resting places; in fact, though they're only a few miles apart from each other, the Schuylkill River runs between them.

West Laurel Hill was founded in 1869 by John Jay Smith, and the privately-owned cemetery remains under the guidance of his direct descendants. The property spans almost 200 acres of land nothing like the sprawling, flat fields of modern cemeteries. Instead, Smith chose this area specifically for its hilly terrain and mature growth, more of a picturesque park ideal for relaxing visits than mere land for burying bodies. This decision was a reflection of the public's new interest in large public parks, which had only just been conceived around the mid-19th century.

Today, the grounds of West Laurel Hill are even more enchanting, enhanced with more than 150 years' worth of sculpture and elaborate mausoleums. Even if you're typically leery of cemeteries and graveyards, you'll most likely find the experience here quite different. And do spend time with the graves because there are dozens of notable names engraved in stone here.

You couldn't possibly visit every grave of interest in a single day, but West Laurel Hill was the world's first cemetery to map its entire property in an app, giving you a headstart at reaching your top choices. And you'll also be privy to plenty of supplemental materials at many of them. Names here represent influential politicians, artists, publishers, authors, Olympians, actors, scientists, musicians, philanthropists, and more, but we'll whet your appetite with just a taste of some classic American brands who owe their most famous creations to those resting here: Luden's, Campbell's Soup, Tylenol, Stetson, Elmer's Glue, Breyers, and Dietz & Watson.

Address 225 Belmont Avenue, Bala Cynwyd, PA 19004, +1 (610) 668-9900, www.westlaurelhill.com | Getting there By car, take I-76 W to Exit 341 to Belmont Avenue | Hours Daily, see website for seasonal hours | Tip The Stetson hat may be the symbol of the American West today, but it originated in Philadelphia. You'll find 1225Raw Sushi and Sake Lounge in the former Stetson headquarters still bearing the name over the door (1225 Sansom Street, www.1225raw.com).

106__Whispering Benches
Share your secrets in public

The existence of the Smith Memorial Arch is no secret to anyone who's entered West Fairmount Park. But it contains a couple of oddities worth noting, one of which you can actively experience yourself. The monumental limestone structure serves as a gateway to the park and features 15 bronzes primarily of Pennsylvanians who served in the American Civil War. Commissioned specifically to honor the state's military heroes, the monument's chief oddity is that one of its most prominent figures is conspicuously *not* a war veteran, and that's the one of the memorial's benefactor, Richard Smith, who is additionally honored in the work's official name.

Smith was a wealthy and influential Philadelphian, who served in the First Continental Congress (representing New Jersey, though) and later bequeathed $500,000 to the city for the creation of this war memorial, leaving the design to an architect and the artist selection to what would become the Association for Public Art. In contemporary value, this donation translates to around $15 million for what was regarded as one of the most epic monuments of its time, so we can't entirely begrudge him the right to be memorialized himself.

The Arch is certainly worth exploring for its historic and artistic values alone, but there's a bit of fun to be had here too, and you'll need to bring a buddy to experience it. Take a seat at one end of one of the long, curved benches mirroring the monument's two main structures and place your partner at the opposite end. Turn your head toward the wall and whisper state secrets, sweet nothings, or limericks, but don't say anything you wouldn't want your companion to hear, because the words will travel clearly along the wall and be received as if you were sitting next to each other, thanks to a physics phenomenon called the parabola effect. Shy people with burning questions, rejoice!

Address Avenue of the Republic, Philadelphia, PA 19104, +1 (215) 546-7550, www.associationforpublicart.org, apa@associationforpublicart.org | Getting there Bus 38 to Concourse Drive & E Road | Hours Unrestricted | Tip A short way up the avenue, the simple fountain across from the Please Touch Museum memorializes one of Fairmount Park's original commissioners, John Welsh (just across from 4231 Avenue of the Republic).

107_Wildlife Refuge
Go birds!

While you may use "Go birds!" for everything from greeting your neighbor to thanking the cashier at Wawa, we're celebrating actual birds this time. The John Heinz National Wildlife Refuge at Tinicum represents a clear conservation victory, safeguarding roughly 1,200 acres of Philadelphia wildlife habitats while opening the natural environments to free public access.

It's important to remember what the land once was, too. Before European arrival, the Lenape lived sustainably around the 5,000-acre marsh that once covered the area, but early colonists quickly drained and filled the region in favor of farms. As Philadelphia sprang up over time, the marsh was ultimately reduced to a mere 200 acres. Recalling history is a critical step in preserving the present and protecting the future, but let's get back to the good news.

Today, the state's largest freshwater tidal marsh is protected by the Wildlife Refuge. This diverse land is home to 10 miles of trails, including the wheelchair accessible Big Boardwalk Loop (under one mile). The most immersive introduction to the Refuge is the 3.5-mile Wetland Loop, where you'll have the best odds of seeing more abundant wildlife. You can also bike this trail (and the others) if it seems too much to walk.

Along the way, you may find anything from foxes and turtles to endangered leopard frogs and rare plants protected in the refuge, but most people come for the birds. More than 300 species have been documented here, and at least 80 of them are known to nest within the property.

Bring a canoe if you feel like doing some fishing, take a free archery lesson (kids 8+ permitted), or take advantage of more than 100 free tours and programs offered throughout the year. Start your day at the Visitor Center, where you can even borrow binoculars and fishing rods, also free.

Address 8601 Lindbergh Boulevard, Philadelphia, PA 19153, +1 (215) 365-3118, www.fws.gov | Getting there Bus 37, 108, 115 to 84th Street & Lindbergh Boulevard | Hours Daily dawn–dusk | Tip Sign up for lessons at the Philadelphia Canoe Club to improve your canoeing skills before visiting the refuge (4900 Ridge Avenue, www.philacanoe.org).

108 William & Letitia Still House

Harriet Tubman stood here – and slept here, too

The very notion that Harriet Tubman actually stood on this particular spot certainly turns heads. However, the reason the William and Letitia Still House was finally recognized and protected by the Philadelphia Register of Historic Places in 2018 has less to do with Tubman and more to do with the Stills themselves.

William Still was a tireless abolitionist who worked for the Pennsylvania Anti-Slavery Society and has been considered second only to Tubman in Underground Railroad operations through the 19th century. At this South Philadelphia house, the Stills sheltered hundreds of people escaping enslavement, including Harriet Tubman herself. Because the marble steps leading to the front door today are likely original to the period of the Stills' residence here, there's a strong chance that Tubman did stand on these precious steps. And she certainly slept within. But back to the Stills.

Not only did the Stills shelter escapees, they did so in the public eye. In one famous escapade later immortalized in the novel *The Price of a Child*, Still was arrested for rescuing a woman and her two children in direct view of the white Southerner claiming ownership of them, assisted by Black dockworkers at the ferry between Philadelphia and Camden. Still has also been pictured in drawings of Henry "Box" Brown being received in Philly after mailing himself to freedom inside a crate that originated in Richmond, Virginia.

We also owe a debt of insight and understanding to Still for leaving behind one of the only first-hand accounts of the Underground Railroad, including a register of all those he assisted and details of many of their escapes, in an 800-page volume. The house was only recently identified through discovery of an advertisement of Letitia Still's dressmaking business in an 1851 newspaper.

Address 625 S Delhi Street, Philadelphia, PA 19147 | Getting there Bus 47M to 9th & Bainbridge Streets | Hours Viewable from the outside only | Tip A historical marker from the National Park Service designates another spot the Stills lived during their time in Philadelphia, from where he published his epic account (244 S 12th Street, www.nps.org).

109__Wonderspaces

A nearly indefinable space

Billed as immersive and interactive art with a full bar, defining Wonderspaces any more succinctly isn't easy, no matter how many times you visit. Housed within Center City's Fashion District Philadelphia, the 24,000-square-foot space hosts 14 exhibitions from international artists, presented on two floors. While some exhibits are regularly phased out to make way for new works, they're all of an absorbing nature, visually and spatially.

Wonderspaces advises the average visit is around 75 minutes, but you're welcome to stay all day once you've entered. At first, you'll be reminded of the eye-popping pop-ups that regularly travel to major cities, bringing Instagram-inspired vignettes perfect for dazzling photos. However, you'll soon realize the goal here is far less about providing a blingy backdrop for your feed as lines of "me-nexts" wait behind you, and much more about drawing you into the engaging environments collectively. Yes, you can still take as many amateur photos as you want; it's just not quite the point.

Unlike the touring pop-ups that threaten limited-time-only access, Wonderspaces is intended to be permanent. Still, it's not quite a museum. You won't find wall-mounted plaques explaining installations or eager docents divulging details. These exhibits are meant to inspire your own curiosity, interpretation, and conversation, which further separates it from the hallowed nature of museums. You can, and should, talk here. In fact, there's a full bar to encourage socialization.

This is a space designed for you to make your own experiential rules, so if you're looking for a hefty dose of order or structure here, you won't find it. Come in with a friend or five, grab a drink and a bite, and choose your own artistic adventure. Welcome to a place for those who have traditionally felt alienated by art (everyone else is welcome, too).

Address 27 N 11th Street, Philadelphia, PA 19107, www.philadelphia.wonderspaces.com | Getting there Bus 44 to Market & 10th Streets; Subway to 11th Street (Market–Frankford Line) | Hours Wed–Fri noon–10pm, Sat 10am–10pm, Sun 10am–8pm | Tip The Fabric Workshop and Museum is a contemporary art museum with far more than fabric, just a five-minute walk from here (1214 Arch Street, www.fabricworkshopandmuseum.org).

110__Wood Street Steps
Step into the past and toward Utopia

Many forget that William Penn's original plans for the state, and especially for Philadelphia, stemmed from a religious experiment. An ardent Quaker, who had been kicked out of school, beaten by his father, and twice imprisoned before making his way across the Atlantic, Penn believed he could create a community based on equality and tolerance, governed by love rather than coercion. Many of his designs were based on simplicity and ease of access rather than grandeur and exclusion, and the city is still famous for originating the simple grid layout of streets that others have emulated since. But most other reminders of Penn's early planning have vanished, and our collective memory of his influence has generally gone with them.

If you take a walk to Front Street, about halfway between Callowhill and Vine, you'll find a quiet set of stone steps in a 10-foot-wide alley. These are among the very few physical remnants of Penn's extensive efforts, and they sat unmarked and largely unnoticed until 2013. They're not particularly useful anymore, as no one really *needs* to travel this alley today, but the Delaware River used to border Water Street (does the name make more sense now?), and these steps provided public access to the riverfront. Penn believed that all citizens deserved access to the water, not just the landowners on its banks, and constructed a series of ten stairways that cut through private property to open the space to all.

These are the last of the ten and are believed to have been replaced, though the timing is unknown. For centuries it was believed the originals were wood, but more recently unearthed records show Penn actually ordered stone steps, so these ones may actually date to the late 17th century. Today, they serve as a last reminder of Penn's commitment to the public health, wellness, and fairness upon which our city was founded.

Address 324 N Water Street, Philadelphia, PA 19106 | Getting there Bus 25 to Columbus Boulevard & Vine Street | Hours Unrestricted | Tip The Arch Street Friends Meeting House wasn't built until 1803, but the land was deeded to the Friends by William Penn in 1701 as a burial ground. Quakers were buried alongside "Indians, Blacks, and strangers," under policy not repeated by other American groups for centuries (320 Arch Street, www.historicasmh.org).

111 World Café Live

An independent stage for everyone

World Café Live (WCL) was born when live music superfan Hal Real and University of Pennsylvania's WXPN radio station came together to address collective concerns. The radio station, home of the nationally syndicated *World Café* radio program, outgrew its former space, and Real was desperate for a thoughtful venue that offered superior sound and sightlines, comfortable seating, decent food, and, above all, a welcoming atmosphere that attracted musicians. Together, *World Café*, along with the rest of WXPN, moved to its current location, where Real built World Café Live's two-stage musical clubhouse that caters to the varying needs of both emerging and internationally touring artists, with community in mind.

World Café Live's calendar is packed with performances, and the venue has remained true to its welcoming mission, filling its schedule with plenty of free and low-cost shows and events to ensure all Philadelphians can come and experience music here. It's a space as much for the residents as for the visiting acts, and WCL additionally works with public schools to offer music education and enrichment experiences to keep Philly's creative spirit incubating. The venue also hosts professional music workshops for people with both physical and cognitive disabilities. Regardless of who you are, if you love live music, this space is for you. And if you're a musician yourself, it's also for you, even if you're just beginning (try an open mic night!).

The Lounge, WCL's restaurant, is a top dining experience, whether you're here for a performance or not. But keep in mind that it's occasionally open only to ticket holders. You'll also find select menus from The Lounge available during many performances, even standing-room-only shows. Ready to give it a try? There's a free concert every Friday at noon, and it's broadcast live on the radio. Come be a part of it!

Address 3025 Walnut Street, Philadelphia, PA 19104, +1 (215) 222-1400,
www.worldcafelive.com, boxoffice-phl@worldcafelive.com | Getting there Bus 42
to Walnut & 30th Streets, or 21, 42 to Chestnut & 31st Streets | Hours Box Office
Tue–Sat 10am–10pm & during events | Tip For more live music and meals, try
Chris' Jazz Café, the longest continuously operating jazz café in Philly history
(1421 Sansom Locust Street, www.chrisjazzcafe.com).

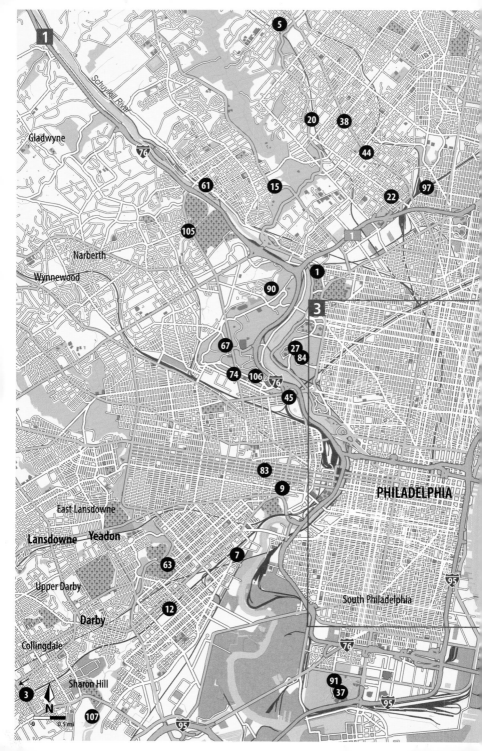

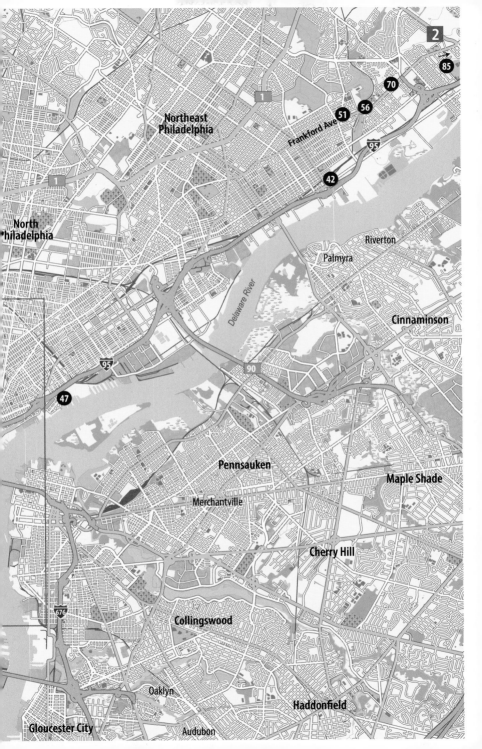

Jo-Anne Elikann
**111 Places in New York
That You Must Not Miss**
ISBN 978-3-95451-052-8

Evan Levy, Rachel Mazor,
Joost Heijmenberg
**111 Places for Kids in New York
That You Must Not Miss**
ISBN 978-3-7408-1218-8

Wendy Lubovich, Ed Lefkowicz
**111 Museums in New York
That You Must Not Miss**
ISBN 978-3-7408-0379-7

Leslie Adatto, Clay Williams
**111 Rooftops in New York
That You Must Not Miss**
ISBN 978-3-7408-0905-8

Joe DiStefano, Clay Williams
**111 Places in Queens
That You Must Not Miss**
ISBN 978-3-7408-0020-8

John Major, Ed Lefkowicz
**111 Places in Brooklyn
That You Must Not Miss**
ISBN 978-3-7408-0380-3

Kevin C. Fitzpatrick Joe Conzo
**111 Places in the Bronx
That You Must Not Miss**
ISBN 978-3-7408-0492-3

Wendy Lubovich, Jean Hodgens
**111 Places in the Hamptons
That You Must Not Miss**
ISBN 978-3-7408-0751-1

Andréa Seiger, John Dean
**111 Places in Washington
That You Must Not Miss**
ISBN 978-3-7408-1560-8

Kaitlin Calogera, Rebecca Grawl,
Cynthia Schiavetto Staliunas
**111 Places in Women's
History in Washington**
That You Must Not Miss
ISBN 978-3-7408-1590-5

Allison Robicelli, John Dean
**111 Places in Baltimore
That You Must Not Miss**
ISBN 978-3-7408-0158-8

Kim Windyka, Heather Kapplow,
Alyssa Wood
**111 Places in Boston
That You Must Not Miss**
ISBN 978-3-7408-1558-5

Amy Bizzarri, Susie Inverso
**111 Places in Chicago
That You Must Not Miss**
ISBN 978-3-7408-1030-6

Amy Bizzarri, Susie Inverso
**111 Places for Kids in Chicago
That You Must Not Miss**
ISBN 978-3-7408-0599-9

Michelle Madden, Janet McMillan
**111 Places in Milwaukee
That You Must Not Miss**
ISBN 978-3-7408-1643-8

Sandra Gurvis, Mitch Geiser
**111 Places in Columbus
That You Must Not Miss**
ISBN 978-3-7408-0600-2

Floriana Petersen, Steve Werney
**111 Places in San Francisco
That You Must Not Miss**
ISBN 978-3-7408-1698-8

Laurel Moglen, Julia Posey,
Lyudmila Zotova
**111 Places in Los Angeles
That You Must Not Miss**
ISBN 978-3-7408-0906-5

Harriet Baskas, Cortney Kelley
**111 Places in Seattle
That You Must Not Miss**
ISBN 978-3-7408-1219-5

Katrina Nattress, Jason Quigley
**111 Places in Portland
That You Must Not Miss**
ISBN 978-3-7408-0750-4

Cristyle Egitto, Jakob Takos
**111 Places in Palm Beach
That You Must Not Miss**
ISBN 978-3-7408-1695-7

Dana DuTerroil, Joni Fincham,
Daniel Jackson
**111 Places in Houston
That You Must Not Miss**
ISBN 978-3-7408-1697-1

Dana DuTerroil, Joni Fincham,
Sara S. Murphy
**111 Places for Kids in Houston
That You Must Not Miss**
ISBN 978-3-7408-1372-7

Philip D. Armour, Susie Inverso
**111 Places in Denver
That You Must Not Miss**
ISBN 978-3-7408-1220-1

Jennifer Bain
**111 Places in Ottawa
That You Must Not Miss**
ISBN 978-3-7408-1388-8

Jennifer Bain, Christina Ryan
**111 Places in Calgary
That You Must Not Miss**
ISBN 978-3-7408-0749-8

Elizabeth Lenell-Davies, Anita
Genua, Claire Davenport
**111 Places in Toronto
That You Must Not Miss**
ISBN 978-3-7408-0257-8

Photo Credits

Assembly (ch. 4): Image courtesy of Assembly Rooftop Lounge

Eternal Performance (ch. 34): Photo courtesy of The Philadelphia Orchestra and Kimmel Cultural Campus

First Person Arts (ch. 39): Image courtesy of First Person Arts

Hamilton Garden (ch. 50): Photo courtesy of The Philadelphia Orchestra and Kimmel Cultural Campus

Jazz Attack (ch. 53): Photo taken by Bill He

Painted Bride (ch. 71): Photograph by Manuel Alé Vasquez (top); Photograph by LaNeshe Miller-White (bottom), Caitlin Green (left) and Ani Gavino dancing in "Grace Period" (2021)

Pulse Fountain (ch. 76): Photograph by Sean O'Neill-Arup, courtesy of Studio Echelman

The Rosenbach (ch. 82): Photos by Ryan Brandenberg

Surgical Amphitheater (ch. 95): Courtesy Pennsylvania Hospital Historic Collections, Philadelphia

W Hotel WET Deck Bar (ch. 103): Image courtesy of W Hotel Wet Deck Bar

Art Credits

From the Mountains; Become the Wind (ch. 30): Vinyl Mural Installation by Andréa Grasso

Artwork (ch. 59): Isaiah Zagar

Meet Me at the Trash Yard 2022 (ch. 71): Mehgan Abdel-Moneim. Milk crates, magnets, Velcro, plastic containers, assorted material. Dimensions variable.

Pulse, Philadelphia, PA Green Line Phase, 2018 (ch. 76): Janet Echelman

Body Paint (ch. 109): Memo Akten

Thanks first to the incredibly diverse Philadelphians whose contributions to the city make up the chapters within this book, and to all those who took so many pains to bring to life their own stories and the stories of others who came before them. Among the many champions of Philly's lesser-known tales and most fascinating current residents, Cara Schneider Bongiorno's infinite passion for, and limitless knowledge of the city and its people saved this book on more than one occasion. It would not exist without her.

It also would not exist without its editor, Karen Seiger, not just for her editorial skill and curatorial guidance, but most especially for her genuine enthusiasm and her indefatigable diplomacy in weathering many a meltdown. Thank you both for your many insights and your endless generosity of patience.

A most special thank you to my partner, Jeffrey Panko, for the constant support and encouragement needed to keep digging and complete this project properly, and for letting me ramble to a New Yorker about so many Philadelphia tidbits for so very many months. I know in your heart you've accepted that our soft pretzels are better than yours, and if that's not devotion, I don't know what is. Thank you for letting me do what I love.

Thanks also to Eric Brooke for the brainstorming and scouting missions; to my favorite teacher, Jan Diers, for one of my most vivid early memories of Philadelphia and for inspiring me to spend my life discovering not just my hometown but the entire world; and to my parents, who have no idea why I do what I do but support it anyway. Finally, not a thanks, but a humble acknowledgment that Philadelphia stands on land unjustly taken from the Lenape, who have cared for this land for more than 10,000 years and to whom the rest of us owe an insurmountable debt.

Brandon Schultz is a world traveler, author, writer and water ice lover who grew up in Greater Philadelphia. He currently travels year-round but is based in Brooklyn, New York. Follow him on Instagram @thebrandonalexandr.

Lucy Baber is a Philadelphia-based photographer and small business owner. In addition to photography, Lucy is also a Mindset Coach, podcast host of *Midlife Plot Twists*, and mom to two boys. Known for her social justice photo project, "100 Black Dads," Lucy uses photography to capture meaningful connections and to give back to the local community. www.lucybaberphotography.com